17 ⁹⁵

THE EAGLES ROAR!

The Eagles Roar!

A FIGHTER PILOT'S STORY OF WORLD WAR II WITH THE AMERICAN EAGLE SQUADRON

By

BYRON KENNERLY
As told to Graham Berry

. . . .

With an Introduction by
CAPTAIN CHARLES SWEENY

. . . .

ZENGER PUBLISHING CO., INC.
P.O. BOX 9883 ● WASHINGTON, D.C. 20015

Library of Congress Cataloging in Publication Data

Kennerly, Byron.
   The Eagles Roar!

   Reprint of the ed. published by Harper, New York.

   1. World War, 1939-1945—Aerial operations, British. 2. World War, 1939-
1945—Personal narratives, American. 3. Kennerly, Byron. 4. Great Britain.
Royal Air Force. Eagle Squadron—Biography. 5. Fighter pilots—United
States—Biography. 6. Fighter pilots—Great Britain—Biography. I. Berry,
Graham, 1909- joint author. II. Title.
D786.K4 1979   940.54'49'41   79-20679
ISBN 0-89201-069-X

Printed in the United States of America

*To American fighter pilots of the
second World War, and especially
to those Eagle Squadron pilots who
led them into the fight.*

INTRODUCTION

THE EAGLE FLYING CORPS of which three squadrons are actually in service on the European front with the Royal Air Force is the grandson in direct line of the Escadrille Lafayette of glorious memory. It was born in France, almost stillborn, in the early spring of 1940. Orphaned, it found a home in England and has paid for its board.

In November, 1939, at the conclusion of negotiations between Edouard Daladier, French Prime Minister, and myself, looking toward the organization of a "Division Etrangère," which was to be formed from regiments of the Foreign Legion, and the command of which I was to assume, General Armengaud, former commander-in-chief of the French Air Corps and my old chief in Morocco, suggested that the greatest service I could undertake at that time was to organize another Escadrille Lafayette with American

flyers after the model of the original one, founded in
1916 by Norman Prince with the assistance of William Thaw and others. General Armengaud pointed
out that the war was very dull; it was usually referred
to as a "phony war." He said that if this continued,
the French nation would become indifferent, that
the only thing Frenchmen could not stand was ennui.
The arrival of American flyers to form another squadron to carry on the glorious traditions of their elder
brothers of 1916-1918 would shake France out of her
lethargy. This appeared so logical that, without further discussion, the plan was adopted. Early in December I left France for Canada.

Many obstacles soon cropped up. The more apparent ones were the Neutrality Law and the attitude
of hostility assumed by a large and influential part
of the American Press. For months I was hounded
like a criminal. I began to have a friendly feeling
for Baby-Face Nelson.

The more real obstacle was the complete apathy of
the American people. Two men, to whom I shall
never be grateful enough, stepped forward at this
time. Without the sympathy and aid of J. Everett
Weddle of Los Angeles and Edwin T. (Ted) Parsons
of Hollywood, one of the most brilliant members of the original Escadrille Lafayette, nothing
would have been accomplished.

Finally the first volunteers reported to me in Canada on April 13th, 1940, and left for France. They were Thomas J. McBride and Vernon Charles Keough. Between then and the tenth of May thirty-two men in all left for and arrived in France. Of these, four were killed and nine are prisoners in Germany. The following men escaped from France and formed the nucleus of the Eagle Flying Corps:

> Newton Anderson
> Vernon Charles Keough
> Michael Luczkow
> Andrew Mamedoff
> Virgil Wilson Olson
> Eugene Quimby Tobin

After the fall of France we, who understood the danger, were very apprehensive of the effect on England. Would she carry on, or would the English people, in face of the seeming impossibility of effective resistance, decide to make the best terms possible? If this should happen we felt that our own country would be in grave danger. I lunched with Constantine Brown, foreign editor of the *Washington Star*, on June 29, 1940, who suggested that the organization of an American Squadron to serve in England might buck up English morale. Thus Great Britain would stay in the war long enough to allow the American people to awaken to the danger. He even consented to make the first necessary contacts.

Early in July, 1940, my nephew, Charles Sweeny, cabled me from London that some of the men of my French Squadron had arrived there and were trying to enlist in the Royal Air Force. The British Government, it appeared, were hesitating about accepting such a small number, but if I could guarantee to furnish the men, the organization of an American Squadron of the Royal Air Force would be authorized.

By August the first men were already on the way, thanks to the efforts of Everett Weddle. On August 29, 1940, Squadron Leader W. E. G. Taylor, Pilot Officer Robert Sweeny, Jr., and I left for England. One day in September Sir Archibald Sinclair, Secretary of State for Air, announced to the assembled American newspaper correspondents that the First Eagle Squadron was considered formed from that date. It had been so christened by my brother, Robert Sweeny.

The following men were listed as members:—

Allen, Luke Elbert
Anderson, Newton
Ayer, John Butler
Bateman, Charles Edward

Bono, Victor Robert
Daymond, Gregory Augustus
Donahue, Arthur Gerald
Goddard, Stanley Earl
Haaren, Paul Joseph
Holton, Oliver Garfield
Kennerly, Byron
Keough, Vernon Charles
Kolendorski, Stanley Michael
LaGuardia, Harry
Leckrone, Philip Howard
Luczkow, Michael
McGinnis, James Leland
Mamedoff, Andrew
Moore, Richard Arthur
Olson, Virgil Wilson
Orbison, Edwin Ezell
Peterson, Chesley Gordon
Provenzano, Peter Benjamin
Satterlee, Dean
Sullivan, Ira Lee
Tobin, Eugene Quimby
Whitehead, Charles Barnett and
Taylor, W.E.G., designated Squadron Leader
Sweeny, Robert, Jr., Adjutant.

INTRODUCTION

The following Monday the men listed below reported to me and the Squadron began to function. The other men on the above list were at school or attached to other services, Coastal Command, Bombing, Ocean Patrol.

Squadron Leader Taylor
Pilot Officer Sweeny, Adjutant
and the following pilots:—
Pilot Officer Allen
Pilot Officer Donahue
Pilot Officer Keough
Pilot Officer Leckrone
Pilot Officer Mamedoff
Pilot Officer Tobin

At the same time Squadron Leader Walter Churchill, D.S.O., D.F.C., reported as instructor. This was a very fortunate choice. Churchill has great understanding and knowledge of men. Vice Air Marshal Richard Saul had recommended him. I can never be too grateful.

The above named men, with the exception of Donahue, were the original members of the Eagle Squadron. Donahue had served in an English Squadron and had been shot down. He came to me from the hospital. Within a few days he was transferred to his old Squadron at his own request. I hated to see him go. He is a mean little guy, with more poetry than meanness in his make-up. I saw in him the makings of an excellent Squadron Leader. I tried to stop his transfer, kicked like a base steer, but it did me no good.

The costs of the operation were borne for much the larger part by my brother, Robert Sweeny, of New York and London. The smaller part was furnished by myself.

CHARLES SWEENY

Late Group Captain, Royal Air Force.

TABLE OF CONTENTS

ILLUSTRATIONS

[xvii]

THE EAGLES ROAR!

Chapter I

THERE'S SOMETHING IN THE AIR

SOMEWHERE over northern England an American flag has been waving its defiance at the totalitarian world since November, 1940. The flag marks the home base of the Eagle Squadron, R.A.F., the first all-American combat unit to see action in the second World War.

I was fortunate enough to be one of the sixteen · pilots posted to the squadron when it was formed. I saw it grow in strength and finally take its place beside England's hard-hitting interceptor squadrons.

This book is the account of my experiences before and after the Eagle Squadron was organized. But if it were only that, there would not be much to write about. So, as much as censorship will allow, this also is the story of my war buddies, how they trained, how they fought, and how some of them died.

Who were these pilots? They were college students, engineers, construction workers, farmers, crop-dusting and commercial flyers. One was a stunt para-chute jumper. All of them had two things in common. They loved to fly. They loved the freedom which flying symbolizes.

Before we go further I will warn you that the stepped-up drama of air war fiction is missing in this story. In the first place my part in the war was not spectacular. In the second place this is not fiction. Also, since truth often is stranger than fiction, you may run across some incidents that are hard to believe. That is, unless you have been in a combat zone and understand that seemingly impossible things suddenly can become almost commonplace.

All right, and now who is this guy who is going to describe the most eventful months of his life? First of all, as a youngster I had no more than the average fellow's desire to fly. In my native state of Kansas and later when the family moved to Oklahoma, I didn't even have the average fellow's schooling. The desire to "see America first" was too strong. When I was twelve I ran away to Texas. On that jaunt I had the presence of mind to wear four pairs of trousers and four shirts, for it was winter. Less forethought was shown in financing the venture. All I had was one dime when I climbed off the cowcatcher of a freight train in Amarillo.

By the time I was sixteen I had left home four times to rove over most of the southwestern United States. I piloted a truck in the Smackover, Arkansas, oil boom, and drove a team in Seminole, Oklahoma. I rode into Seminole in a baggage car that carried seven coffins. They had been ordered after a particularly festive week-end there. Bullets flew pretty thick in those days. Perhaps some of these early experiences later helped me to fly a Hurricane armed with eight machine guns.

When I was sixteen, my family moved to Oregon, where I worked in the lumber mills. There I became an "ace." Not as a flyer but as a block-setter. He's the fellow who runs the big, raw logs through the growling saws. For several years in the Northwest woods I drove tractors and trucks and ran mining dredges. It was here I acquired the nickname of Jack. The fellows I worked with never could remember to call me Byron. When things boomed in the oil fields of Long Beach, California, I moved south, driving more trucks and building roads for them.

While I was drifting from one job to another, unconsciously I was following one star, if you could call machinery by so poetical a name. Whatever or

[3]

wherever the job, my working partners were trucks, tractors, road scrapers, buzz saws, dredges. Like thousands of other American fellows, I learned to understand them and to respect them. Perhaps that was why, when I paid two dollars and a half to take my first airplane ride at Seal Beach, I decided to take up flying. To me an airplane was and still is the ultimate in machinery.

I'll never forget that first flight. We took off down wind in a fog. The pilot yelled to me that he was showing me "the wrong way to fly." You don't take off down wind unless you have to. Even a sea gull heads into the wind before hopping off. But even the wrong way to fly was to me the right way to travel. It was a thrill when we roared up through the fog into the brilliance of sunlight. I felt like a god, enjoying the grandeur of a sparkling sky that was denied me as a mere mortal in the shrouded land below.

The next day I took my first flying lesson. Unlike some of the boys who were ready to solo after four or five hours of instruction, it took me nine hours and sixteen minutes. I worked on aerobatics and spent six dizzy hours in a Link Trainer. You can do anything in one of these that you can in a plane except take it off the ground. You sit in it with a hood covering the cockpit and learn to fly "blind," or only with instruments. The trainer will spin, dive and climb, maneuvering on a universal joint. If you don't think you can get woozy "flying" one, try it.

Then came the war and I followed closely the accounts of the major role airplanes were playing. I learned that England needed flyers. I knew that my experience—I had built up 185 hours of flying time—wouldn't qualify me as a fighter or bomber pilot. And all my time was in very light airplanes, far different from powerful war planes. But England was willing to train fellows with some flying experience.

I made the biggest decision of my life, deciding to apply to the Royal Air Force for the job of fighter pilot. I knew my physical reactions were fast. And a fighter pilot, above all else, needs to react quickly. I didn't want to become a bomber pilot. I had the idea that when a fighter pilot got too old, he was shifted to a bomber. Actually, it takes more experience to handle a multimotored bomber than the lighter pursuit ship.

Having saved a little money, I was able to fly by airliner to New York. There I interviewed an R.A.F. official and was told to go to Ottawa, Canada, for a flight test. If I passed, I would receive a commission in the Royal Air Force as pilot officer, the equivalent to a second lieutenant in our air force. I asked a question that was vital to me: If a man joined the R.A.F., would he lose his American citizenship? I was assured he wouldn't.

Confident I could pass a test in any light ship, I took an airliner to Ottawa. There I underwent the toughest physical examination I ever had. For the first time in my life my eyes were dilated with belladonna. I hoped I wouldn't have to pass the flight test with my vision blurred by this medicine. The Canadian doctor assured me the blurring would pass off shortly. Not satisfied with examining me from the outside, the doctor took x-ray pictures of my lungs. Although I felt in perfect shape, I began to believe that if this examination kept on, he was sure to find something wrong with me. But he didn't.

The R.A.F. put me up at the Chateau Laurier, one of the most luxurious of Canada's hotels. In the swanky lobby I met an American from Milwaukee who introduced himself as John Ayer. He was an athletic looking fellow with red hair and mustache. He was up here for the same purpose as I, and said there were several other American boys in Ottawa signing up. John had had some military experience as a reserve officer.

It was August 2, 1940, the day scheduled for my

flight test. I felt a bit nervous, having just learned that one American with 800 flying hours, more than four times mine, had flunked it.

Arriving at the airport, or airdrome as they are called here and in England, my uneasiness wasn't eased any to discover that, instead of the light airplanes I was used to, the hop was to be in a husky, American-built Harvard, an advanced trainer. The fastest plane I had flown was a Ryan, with a top speed of 125 M.P.H. These bright yellow Harvards could roll up to 210.

I met Flight Lieutenant McA. of the Royal Canadian Air Force, who got me a parachute, helmet and goggles. We arrived beside a Harvard.

"Jump in Kennerly, it won't bite you," McA. grinned, noticing my hesitancy.

I scrambled into the deep front cockpit to be confronted with a confusing assortment of instruments, many of which I knew nothing about. The flight lieutenant showed me how to work the flaps, the boost pressure and retractable undercarriage. I'd never flown a plane with flaps, those movable fins at the trailing edge of the wings that, when lowered, act as brakes in a landing. As for the boost pressure and retractable undercarriage, they were just a couple of more things to learn about in too much of a hurry.

[7]

The officer got in back and took us off. The roar on the take-off was terrific. Because of the high tip-speed of the propeller, the Harvard is one of the noisiest planes in the sky.

Being a trainer, the plane of course had dual controls, and I followed the pilot through on them to get the feel of the ship. After we'd climbed to 2,000 feet, McA. told me to take over and fly straight and level. As soon as I started flying her, I lost my nervousness. She flew easily and the only difference I noticed from other planes I'd flown was that the controls were a little stiffer. That was because the added speed caused increased pressure on ailerons, rudder and elevators.

McA. took over and made some climbing and gliding turns. I repeated the maneuvers, which brought out a pilot's air sense and co-ordination. McA. took us over in a loop. I took her over the next time. This showed a man's sense of orientation and feeling for pressure. If you loop correctly, you don't even need a safety belt to keep you in your seat. But don't try it without one!

Then we did wing overs, lazy eights, and slow rolls. In the roll you keep the ship's nose pointed at some object on the horizon. Then you just roll the wings around, keeping the nose on the objective. Next came chandelles, climbing turns that are good for a fighter pilot to know about when he's taking evasive action from a diving enemy. We went through some more maneuvers, including high speed stalls. After forty-five minutes of it, McA. said over the speaking tube, "Jolly good ride. Let's go down and land."

Unfamiliar with the country, I previously had spotted a canal near the airport, found it, followed it to the field and landed. McA. took me to lunch and I felt I had the test about buttoned up. He told me that because I was thirty-one, eight or nine years older than the average age of fighter pilots, he was putting me through an extra stiff test.

After lunch I made two more landings and take-offs with him. Then he ordered me to take her up alone for forty-five minutes. I did and for nearly an hour the plane and I cavorted in the sky. I kept within a ten-mile radius of the field, not wanting to get lost. That would have been a beautiful way to wreck my chances of getting into the R.A.F.

When I finally came down and taxied to the line, McA. greeted me with, "Fine, Kennerly. You'll do as a fighter pilot."

Those were the most welcome words I had ever heard!

Chapter II

PASSENGERS, POTATOES, AND GUNPOWDER

I TOOK the train back to Ottawa feeling mighty good. I'd cleared the first hurdle and England didn't seem so far away now. But I still had to pass the character test. And it was a stiff one. I talked to one fellow who had passed the flight examination a hundred per cent. But in checking up on him the British discovered he had passed one small bad check against his own father. The Air Ministry rejected him. The fellow was broken-hearted. While England needed fighter pilots badly, she wanted no one with any criminal tendencies, no matter how small the tendency.

I reported at the British Air Ministry headquarters in Ottawa and was subjected to an intense grilling. I submitted letters of recommendation from the mayor, police chief, and district attorney of Klamath

Falls, Oregon, my old home town. A sharp-eyed intelligence officer told me to wait three days while my story was checked by telegram.

As I left his office, certain this had been a greater ordeal than the flight test, I spotted four fellows coming down the corridor. From the way they wore their clothes and from the fact two of them were suntanned, I knew they were Americans. We introduced ourselves. They, too, wanted to become fighter pilots and were going through the check-up mill.

The tall, cotton-headed member of the quartet gave his name as "Pete" Peterson. His real name was Chesley Gordon Peterson. He had just graduated from Brigham Young University, Utah. He had the look of a flyer about him. He introduced me to Richard Arthur ("Jim") Moore, a tall, dark fellow who claimed to be part Indian. "You can't beat Hitler at Fort Worth, so I want to go over," Jim said. The other two fellows were Californians. James Leland McGinnis, an aeronautical engineer, was from Hollywood. He looked more like a well dressed business man than a pilot. Then there was Charles Edward Bateman, a well built, good looking chap, a former University of California student. He had lived in San Gabriel, a few miles from Pasadena, my last home while I was working on a dam construction job. We'd almost been neighbors. Of course I didn't know then that these fellows were to become my buddies in the Eagle Squadron.

They all had considerable flying time in their log books. A log, of course, is a little book a pilot carries with a complete record of all his flights.

I returned to my luxurious room at the chateau, where Ayer and I celebrated our passing the flight test. We didn't do too much celebrating for I wasn't "in" until the character references had been okayed.

Three days later I got a ticket to England, together with instructions and sealed orders that were not to be opened until we were at sea. I was "in"! We weren't to get uniforms until we reached an operational training unit "somewhere in England."

Altogether I stayed at the chateau a week and a half. I had all my expenses paid, plus five dollars a day spending money. Pilots had stayed there with no limit on expenses. However, two or three champagne parties had caused the British government to reduce the "sky's the limit" policy to the generous daily allowance.

We did considerable sightseeing and found the Canadian people were taking the war very seriously. There was a big difference in public attitude here and a few miles away in America.

The morning we pilots were to leave for Montreal and an east Canadian port to embark, I relied too much on the clock in the chateau lobby. It was an hour too slow, so I missed the train. Rushing to the air ministry office, I requested the use of a plane to fly to Montreal. The ministry instead arranged for my passage aboard an airliner, which got me in Montreal two hours ahead of the train.

Taking a taxi to the station, who should I run into but Ayer, who had driven down by automobile and had just put his car in a garage. He had motored over originally from the United States. With time on our hands, we decided to see some of the city. It was two o'clock in the afternoon.

Strolling by a swanky night club we saw the picture of a blonde, in a glass case.

"That's Edith Rogers!" exclaimed Ayer. She was the girl who personally appealed to Franco and thus saved Whitey Dahl from a Spanish firing squad. Ayer had met Whitey, whose life in Spain as a pilot had made him famous, and suggested we go in and see if she was there.

A big guy with an ugly scar over his lip stopped us as we entered the club. Ayer explained he was a good friend of Edith Rogers' husband. We got by Tarzan, who told us Edith was conducting a dress rehearsal and would be glad to see us. There was lots of glass paneling around and some fancy chandeliers hung from the domed ceiling. A bartender was fussing about behind a long bar.

We didn't take time to study the architecture or interior decorations, for ahead of us on a dimly lighted stage was Edith, dressed in a tight-fitting white evening gown, directing a half dozen chorus girls in a dance. Just offstage a disheveled pianist was pounding out unrecognizable rhythm.

John pranced onto the stage and stopped the show, introducing himself and beckoning to me. Edith greeted us as if we were old friends. Telling the pianist to "take over," she flung a fur coat over her shoulders and ushered us to the bar. After she had introduced us to a powerful concoction called a "zombie," I began to wonder whether I was going to miss another train that day.

We had a long talk about Whitey, who was training pilots in Canada. John gave her every scrap of information he could remember about him, and some he could not. She told us about her work in the show business. My watch hands were closing in on four o'clock, but Edith told us not to worry, she'd get us aboard the train.

John and I finished our second zombie apiece and

Edith helped extricate us from the club, which some- how had become cluttered with furniture and other obstructions. We climbed into her Cadillac limousine and she drove us to the station.

For being such a perfect hostess, we tried to kiss her good-by, but had to be satisfied with handshakes. We climbed aboard the train, waving to her. The touching scene made a great impression on the five other American pilots, who gathered in the vestibule of our car to watch the farewells. They questioned us closely as to who our lovely date was. John didn't satisfy their curiosity when he winked and passed it off with, "Just an old friend of the family."

The train pulled out. It was a long ride, lasting until next evening. There were seven of us American pilots, including Ayer and the boys I had met at the air ministry and Paul Haaren, who was forty-eight years old. He later joined the Coastal Command. We took over the rear car of the train, waving at towns- folk of villages and cities we passed through. There were four or five girls on the train and we held dances. We acted like a gang of crazy kids. We were all pretty excited about the grand adventure we were undertaking.

We detrained at the coastal port in the evening and hustled directly aboard a big liner, grim appearing in her gray and black war paint. She was a 24,000-ton vessel. I was glad she was a fast ship, able to make about twenty knots, for this is faster than submarines can travel.

Instead of bands playing, people cheering and confetti flying, everything was quiet as we boarded her. Despite the lack of fanfare, everyone was excited, especially us. As I stepped on deck I felt I was almost in England. There were many passengers on board. Besides us, there were contingents of Canadian soldiers and a group of nurses who had brought children from England to Canada for the duration.

As soon as we were aboard, the vessel sailed. I peered at the murky late evening sea to spot some armed escort. There was none. Members of the crew told us the ship had brought over some Nazi prisoners. It was heartening to learn that she had been examined carefully before we sailed to make sure no prisoner had planted a time bomb in her. One of the Nazis had crossed over the ship's boundary into a restricted area near one of her guns; he had been ordered back. The Nazi had just growled. Twice more he was ordered to the prisoner area. Twice more he refused so he was shot where he stood.

For protection the ship carried several machine guns and two bigger ones, one on the bow and one aft. They were combination antiaircraft and antisub guns. I hoped that if we had to use them, we got the enemy before we got a torpedo or bomb. This hope became all the more ardent when I discovered that, in addition to passengers and a large cargo of potatoes, we carried a big assortment of ammunition.

The first three days out, we flyers stayed pretty much to ourselves, talking to members of the crew and the Canadian soldiers, who were a fine lot of fellows. I'd hate to be a Nazi and meet these soldiers in combat. They all were good shots. Most of them having spent their lives in the northern woods, they were able to take care of themselves under any circumstances. Canadians, Americans, Australians and New Zealanders, as far as I have been able to find out, make the best individual fighters in the world. They don't become panicky when left on their own in a tight spot.

On the afternoon of the third day, word ran over the ship a sub had been sighted. We were at full speed ahead, running a zigzag course. I ran to the stern, where sailors already had uncovered and loaded a wicked looking rifle with about a four-inch barrel. It was trained astern. A gray mist hung over the sea, making it impossible to see any distance. The water was choppy with a heavy swell underneath. Far astern and near our wake I saw what appeared to be a stick poking out of the water. It was gray, the same color as the ocean, and was visible only because its gray line cut through an occasional whitecap back of it. It gave me a queer feeling, watching the alert gunners standing by their posts on the heaving deck and two officers at the rail, one with binoculars and the other with a ship's telescope. They were looking at the "stick" too.

Often you can't tell whether you're looking at a sub until you see the fast lengthening wake of a torpedo. Then it may be too late to maneuver out of the way.

We changed course and I could feel the vibrations of the straining engines as we plowed through the rolling Atlantic.

In a few moments the tension eased. If it had been a periscope we spotted, we were too far away to be damaged. A submerged submarine can travel only from seven to eight miles an hour. Even on the surface, we could outrun one. But we couldn't outrun a speedy torpedo. The gun crews and officers kept on the alert for several hours. Often when one sub is sighted it means that more are in the vicinity. They run in schools.

That night the ship held a party. It was Jim

Moore's birthday and we had a special dinner and champagne, with the captain presiding.

The day after we got our first sub alarm, a periscope definitely was sighted off the starboard bow. I could see it plainly, as visibility had improved. There were spots of sunlight on the sea, showing through cloud rifts. Our front as well as rear guns were uncovered. We changed our course away from the ugly periscope. We didn't fire, wanting to slip away if we could. Besides, it might be a British sub. We got away all right. The captain told us he believed we had been through two schools of enemy submarines in the past two days.

The sixth day it got very foggy. This was welcome, making us practically invisible to marauders. Pete and I were in the dining saloon listening to some nurses describe the terrors of bombing raids on civilian populations—which we frankly didn't believe at the time—when we heard the drone of airplane motors. We hurried on deck and peered into the haze.

Headed toward us from the east and not 500 feet above the water was a huge four-motored aircraft that looked a lot like one of our big clipper seaplanes. But instead of sponsons, or stub lower wings which form the undercarriage for take-offs in water, this plane had a fixed strutted and braced float about two thirds of the way out on each wing. As it banked to come around our port side I saw bull's-eyes on the wings and fuselage. Welcome sights! It was a Sunderland flying boat, a patrol bomber and arch enemy of submarines. She circled our ship and I saw flashes of light from her forward cabin. Someone was signaling us with an Aldis lamp, a light that throws a beam only directly ahead. I looked up on our bridge and saw officers signaling back. The Sunderland circled several times, continuing her signals, then wheeled away like a huge graceful buzzard and disappeared into the fog.

Later in the day a Lockheed-Hudson, American-made reconnaissance bomber came over and gave us more signals before veering off. Several more times patrol bombers came over and circled. I knew from this we must be nearing England. We learned we were to reach our destination early next morning. We had been six days in the crossing, which I thought was pretty fast, considering the long and zigzag course we had been forced to take.

We were up bright and early the next day. There was no motor vibration and I knew we must be riding at anchor. Up on deck we got our first view of a west England harbor with a city beyond. From what I saw, I realized that at last we were in the war zone.

Off our starboard bow and jutting up squarely from the calm water were what appeared to be two piers that once had held a bridge. But they weren't piers. They were two halves of a freighter that had been cut cleanly in two. The ship must have been bombed, breaking apart in the middle, the nose sinking to leave the middle sticking up and the stern also going down, leaving the other half of the middle above the water. It looked as if the vessel had been cut in half with a saw, so even was the break.

Motionless in the sky, several thousand feet above the city, hung rows of silvery balloons. They prevented dive-bombing. Their effectiveness was demonstrated by the fact that from where we were anchored I couldn't see any bomb damage in the great expanse of docks fanning out from the city's business district. It was a good sight to see the shores of England and we were impatient to dock. Among several large buildings on the skyline, I could see the spires of one of England's many famous cathedrals.

We were told to get our breakfast because it would be several hours before we docked. After eating we spent three hours watching five mine sweepers comb the harbor, a fleet of tiny vessels in echelon, each pulling about 200 yards of submerged steel cable. To the other end of the cables were fastened hollow tin cylinders more than six feet long. The cylinders travel at about a forty-five-degree angle with the ship's wake, keeping the cable taut. The cable acted as a fine, sharp saw, cutting a submerged mine loose from its anchor cable and allowing the mine to come to the surface, where it could be destroyed by firing a bullet at it and setting it off. A sailor said the front sweeper was the only one that might strike a mine. The next ship in line traveled in the swept waters of the one in front. The third sweeper rode in the swept waters of the second one and so on.

The third boat—they were stretched out quite a way from each other—stopped. In less than a minute there was a puff of smoke and a few hundred yards from it a geyser of water shot up.

After the sweeping was over, we had to wait for high tide. It was after noon when we steamed into the dock. I scanned the line of docks for signs of damage. There were none. Across a river we saw one entire business block wiped out, apparently by bombs with the aid of incendiaries. Soldiers were standing on the dock; they were armed with bayoneted rifles.

We said good-by to the nurses. One of them asked us to visit her in London and meet her husband, who was in the theatrical business. An efficient-looking little British intelligence officer met us, examined our credentials, and directed us to the railroad station.

We walked the few blocks from the pier to the station. The streets were crowded with people. All seemed happy and not the least bothered by the war that the bombing planes had brought to their front yards. The station was very dark inside, blacked out completely. It, too, was filled with people, many of them soldiers and sailors. We had to peer through the darkness at tiny illuminated signs of coffee shops, ticket windows, and train numbers.

As I later discovered was true of all English stations, the trains backed into long sheds attached to the station. The seven of us boarded our train, which soon chugged off for London.

We caught a few glimpses of the English landscape as we sped along. The most unusual thing to us was the lack of advertising signs and directional signposts. They had all been removed. We passed several small concentrations of soldiers and mechanized equipment.

In one village was a group of elderly men, many of them in their sixties and seventies, marching and carrying a strange assortment of guns, including large gauge shotguns. These must be the home guard we had heard about. They were grim-faced gentlemen who took their marching seriously. Parachute troops would have a tough time landing anywhere.

We passed several short caravans of army trucks rolling along the highways. There were few civilian cars, but many bicycles with civilians pedaling them. I saw several sets of concrete abutments on either side of the highways, with stout columns of concrete piled by the roadside. Heavy iron rings were set in them. A British officer told us these were tank traps, that the columns were ready to roll onto the road to block it. On each side of these peculiar emplacements were either ditches or concrete poles set in the ground, fanning out for perhaps ten yards. Newly-laid pavement or cobblestones on the sides of these tank traps were "mined" the officer said. The British certainly looked ready to defend every inch of their tight little isle.

We spotted several concrete blockhouses, with gun slits. These were scattered either near wide sweeps of open ground where attackers would be forced into the open or in places where attackers would have to crowd through narrow defiles.

Several army camps were located near the railroad. Most of them were equipped with small, fast, camouflaged tanks. The beautiful meadows and open fields were scarred with snaky ditches and stubby posts, set twenty to thirty feet apart. The Britishers weren't leaving any spots to be used as landing fields by the Luftwaffe.

It was night time when we pulled into London. We got out of the train and, carrying our grips, headed for a near-by hotel we had heard was good. It was my first experience in a blackout and it was a strange feeling, fumbling through a great strange city in which every light was extinguished. There were quite a few people on the streets and we continually bumped into them. Finally, aftter considerable asking, we arrived at the King's Cross Hotel, where we got reservations. Ayer and I got a room together.

After we had washed some of the travel off our faces and brushed up a bit, we decided to get a bite to eat and take a stroll. We planned not to stray far from the hotel. If we did, we knew we never could find it until daylight. Londoners must have a wonderful sense of direction to find their way around in "blackout" dark. And believe me, that's a very special kind of intense darkness. This sixth sense, we decided, must be developed after living through the famous fogs we heard clung to this land.

Just before Ayer and I left our room we heard a loud knocking. Opening the door we were surprised to see an angry, red-mustached face, looking for all the world like Bairnsfather's Bill.

Before we could ask what he wanted, the owner of the red face stormed in and demanded:

"What's the idea, leavin' the shade up! I should a shot yer light out!"

Wow! We had turned on the light and forgotten to black the room out. I ran to the window, pulled the shade down and shoved the heavy black curtains across it, trying to apologize to the still blustering Britisher.

We told him this was our first night in London and that we had come over to join the R.A.F. This seemed to mollify him and he explained that he was a particularly soft-hearted air raid warden, adding that it was the custom, when a light was discovered from the outside, to take careful aim and shoot it out.

"You know, gentlemen," he said with mock seriousness, " 'Itler promised 'e was goin' ter be in London town by August the fifteenth. 'E's a bit overdue now an' we don't want no welcome lights shinin' for 'im." With this he left us.

Wondering whether we could get any of the food we wanted, we went down to the hotel grill. I decided that Britishers still ate well when one of the best steaks I ever had was put in front of me. The only difference I noticed between meals here and in America was that here butter and sugar were served to each of us individually. We were allowed but three lumps of sugar apiece. As this was more than I ever used at one meal, I felt that no restrictions were being placed on me. The waitress, however, told us many Britishers nearly filled their teacups with sugar and sometimes they felt they were making a real sacrifice, using only three lumps. We had some brussels sprouts. I never could figure out why they were invented and was soon to learn, unfortunately, that they were a staple part of the British diet. The big dinner made us realize we weren't going to lose weight in England, at least as far as food was concerned.

After we had finished we left the brightly lighted hotel dining room to go out into the blackest night I have ever seen. The darkness gave me the same sensation as if a black rug had been thrown over my head. I stood for a moment, blinking at it. I heard the traffic on the street before I saw it. Then, as my eyes became accustomed to the dark, I could see dimmed lights of motor cars moving slowly along. Then there was the glow of pedestrians' cigarettes. Over the rooftops three searchlights lazily swept the sky. There was a dull rumble in the distance. At first

I thought it was traffic. It was antiaircraft fire. The British call it ack-ack or flak or A.A. The antiaircraft guns are known familiarly as archies.

Although I was sorry I hadn't gotten my first glimpse of this great city in daylight to catch something of the magnitude of it, somehow I could feel its great size and could sense its sprawling thousands of buildings and the presence of its eight million inhabitants. It was an uncanny sensation.

We walked along gingerly, occasionally bumping into piles of sandbags and exclaiming "excuse me" before we realized they weren't people. We kept on excusing ourselves, however, because quite often our victims were people. A half-hour of this was enough for us; so we felt our way back to the hotel.

To be certain we did not again offend our air raid warden, when Ayer and I turned in we left the curtains drawn, even after we had turned out the light. We didn't want to take any chances of walking in our sleep and unconsciously snapping on the light.

Chapter III

HE HEILS HITLER

ALTHOUGH we weren't due at the Air Ministry the next morning until ten o'clock, we were up bright and early. We wanted to have time to walk to the ministry building so we could get a daylight glimpse of the world's largest city.

After a healthy breakfast, the seven of us started forth with our suitcases. The streets were pretty well crowded with people on their way to work. There was a good sprinkling of uniforms in the crowd. And the women were wearing their share of them. Most everyone carried a gas mask.

Hanging over the city at the same elevation of about 5,000 feet were herds of barrage balloons. At the edge of a small park there was a big truck with a crew unreeling a cable into the sky. Pulling and jerking at the cable was a balloon, being sent up to join its fellows. It was ascending nose up, a baggy loose rudder dragging behind. As it neared 5,000 feet, the floppy rudder began to stand out awkwardly. It apparently was inflating in the rarefied atmosphere. All the balloons pointed the same way, noses into the wind. I'd heard they sometimes were as tough on R.A.F. pilots as on Nazi bombers. In the industrial zones where coal smoke mixes with fog to form a black soup, British planes sometimes got snagged by a cable. For this reason, and because the balloon officers called their work flying, R.A.F. pilots didn't care for the balloon barrage system. The chief job of the balloons was to prevent Nazi bombers from flying low so they could aim accurately. Attached to trucks which could send them up from any part of the city, the balloons did their job well.

London already had undergone several raids, although the big ones hadn't started. It was several blocks to the Air Ministry and we saw only two buildings that had been hit. One of them must have been badly wrecked, for every scrap of it had been cleared away, leaving a clean "vacant lot" between two other buildings.

All street signs had been removed. Where names of streets or localities had been a part of the name of a store or business firm, these parts had been removed carefully. On several rooftops were machine-gun nests. Sandbag walls guarded windows on first floors.

Aside from the sandbags, the lack of directional signs, and the gas masks, London looked a good deal like a combination of New York and Los Angeles; New York because of the enormous size of the city and Los Angeles because there are no skyscrapers in London either. Both cities spread out instead of up.

As we walked along, rubber-necking like a gang of hicks from "Hog Hollow," I noticed people staring at me. Several women giggled outright.

Finally Jim Moore asked a friendly looking bobby, "Do we look funny to you?"

The bobby obligingly inspected us and stopped when he came to me.

"Well, yes in a way," he nodded at me. "Maybe it's because that gentleman's wearing a straw topper and white shoes. It's not quite the style in London this year."

Good grief, I hadn't thought to change my southern California attire. Jim suggested that I walk toward the next women who laughed as if I thought they were flirting. Two smartly dressed women, hurrying along the street, smiled at me. I started toward them, raising my hat. I never saw people change expressions so quickly. They half sidled away, like skittish colts, and looked across the street. Enough of that game.

We arrived at the Air Ministry building a few

minutes before the appointed time. Sentries were pacing in front of the five-story stone structure that represented the nerve center of the great Royal Air Force. We presented our credentials to a sentry, who escorted us inside where an officer inspected our identification cards. We were introduced to a cordial wing commander, who, in a businesslike office, full of file cases and pictures of aircraft, asked us why we came over to fight for Britain.

We all gave about the same answer: Our two countries and our ways of life were closely tied and we didn't want to see individual rights subordinated to the whims of a dictator. Jim added that no man ever had made him so mad as Hitler and the best way to get a crack at that guy was to join the R.A.F. We expressed our admiration for the air force and its personnel. Then the officer asked us when America was coming into the war. I expressed my conviction we would be in it sooner or later and that we fellows might be called the "advance guard" of the military might of America.

The commander gave us written orders, which instructed us to catch a train at Waterloo Station almost immediately. Six of us were going to an operational training unit in northwest England to learn how to fight in the air. Paul Haaren, who had been with us all this time, was going into the Coastal Command. We bid him good-by. Piling into a taxi, we were rushed to the station.

Hurrying into the building, we climbed aboard a long train just before it pulled out. We'd no more than settled in our compartment when a young British officer with an eyelash mustache popped in and asked, "You're American flyers, aren't you?" As we nodded, he continued, "Thought you might be interested to know we have a Jerry prisoner aboard. An ace pilot, too. Want to meet him?"

Did we! Here was a chance to get a close-up view of the kind of guy we would be apt to run up against in combat. We followed the officer through two cars to a compartment in a third one. He rapped three times and swung the door open. With arms crossed over a muscular chest and a scowl on his handsome, fair-complexioned face, sat the prisoner, staring glumly ahead. A British soldier was seated next to him, his bayoneted rifle barrel resting against the seat, the butt on the floor. The Nazi easily could have reached for the gun. Across from him was another British soldier.

The officer introduced us to Captain T. Learning we were Americans, he looked at us curiously. Then he stood up and shook hands all around as we crowded into the small compartment. He was a fine specimen of a man. His gray uniform was criss-crossed with wrinkles and looked as if the pilot had gone swimming in it. He had a deep cleft in his chin and when he finally smiled, he displayed a set of teeth that would honor any toothpaste ad.

"He's a bit sore," explained the British officer, "because the sailors who rescued him in the Channel pulled off his officer's stripes and iron cross to keep as trinkets. It was rather a poor show and if the blighters are caught, they'll be court-martialed."

"Nah," the German answered in fairly good English, "it is not the custom in my country to strip an officer of his rank and medals when he is taken prisoner."

He seemed not at all grateful that his life had been saved by the men who had made him sore. I gave him a package of American cigarettes. This thawed him out.

He told us he was a captain in the crack Yellow Nose Squadron and had shot down twenty-seven planes. He had been in four campaigns, Polish, Norwegian, French and British. The Yellow Nose Squadron was the top fighter squadron of the Luftwaffe. To remain in the outfit each man had to shoot down a certain number of planes and keep on shooting them down. Yellow Nose pilots flew Messerschmitt

109's, at this time the fastest fighters of the German air force.

"My first trip across the Channel I get shot down. I have to stay in the water two hours and twenty minutes before I am picked up," Captain T. explained, adding ruefully that he was shot down Wednesday and on the following Saturday he was to have been married!

I asked him how he liked Hitler. Immediately he stood up, shot his right hand forward and up, palm out, clicked his heels and said, "Heil Hitler."

We took turns going out to buy him candy and cookies. He ate enough to make an ordinary man sick. Occasionally one of us asked him again what he thought of Hitler. Each time he would rise and go through the "Heil Hitler" ceremony. He didn't seem annoyed at us for this.

"But you say you are Americans," he asked earnestly. "Is America now in the war?"

"No," Pete shook his head. "The six of us here came over to take a hand in the show."

The prisoner looked from one to the other of us, a look of disbelief on his face.

"You mean you are going to fight for the fun of it?" He laughed. "Perhaps it won't be quite the sport you imagine."

He added that aerial combat was a business with

him, a business performed for the fatherland. He had been in the Luftwaffe ten years and had flown since he was twelve.

It was our turn to be surprised. "Yes," he grinned, "there was one loophole in the Versailles Treaty." At the mention of this treaty he frowned. "While Germany was forbidden to build an air force, there were no restrictions against gliding. There were 80,000 gliders in Germany in 1932. I learned to fly in one.

"And," he added confidentially, "you have to know how to fly to handle a glider. It is the purest form of flight. Like a sea gull, you take advantage of wind currents to keep you aloft. You use thermals—rising air currents—to climb."

His keen blue eyes sparkled as he talked about gliding. He forgot he was a prisoner as he described one of the strangest air adventures I ever heard. Later I talked to other captured German airmen and they confirmed this story, which occurred before the war.

Three pilots, friends of Captain T., had been trying to set altitude records in their motorless aircraft. One afternoon they spotted a thunderhead. Of course, under this type of cloud formation there is an updraft of air, a narrow column of it, which whips up into the thunderhead and breaks, spilling over into the cloud much as the crest of a fountain spills.

The three Germans steered their gliders under the cloud, knowing they'd find a thermal. Once in the up-draft, they would circle slowly and be picked right up into the cloud. They got into the thermal, all right, and began circling. Checking their altimeters, however, they were shocked to learn they were rising at nearly 200 miles an hour!

It was too late to do anything and they were hurled far up into the cloud. When they reached the turbulence area, the air was so rough that even the sturdy wooden gliders couldn't take it and broke apart.

One pilot was hurled through the wooden side of his ship, the wood severing the shoulder straps of his parachute harness. Not realizing the straps had been cut, he pulled the rip cord and the parachute flared open. Had he been dropping head first, the 'chute would have pulled him out of his thigh straps and he'd have fallen to his death. But he was dropping feet first. When the 'chute took hold of the air, the entire strain in the ensuing jerk was placed on his leg straps. He was nearly split apart. He began suffering severe hemorrhages.

He descended under the cloud, but his troubles weren't over. A strong cross wind caught him and relentlessly carried him into the up-draft. It was too rough to steer away from the dangerous thermal by pulling the shrouds and spilling air from his parachute canopy. He might have collapsed the 'chute and it would have been all over but the funeral. He got caught in the thermal and was whisked upward at a terrific speed. When he reached the turbulence area, he was hurled over the top of the "air fountain" and began his second descent. After he descended below the cloud again, the same strong cross wind caught him and carried him into the thermal.

Suffering terrifically all the while, he made three round trips through that cloud. At the end of the third trip, the turbulent air tossed him over the other side of the thermal. This time, after he got below the cloud, the cross wind carried him away from the thermal. He landed safely. The other two fellows had landed safely long before and were horrified when they saw him go up into the clouds the third time.

Captain T., apparently glad to find fellow airmen to talk to, went on volubly about gliders, describing how Britain might be invaded by glider-borne troops. He pointed out that it required only three-and-a-half horsepower for a power plane to tow a single-place glider in level flight. Thus a powerful bomber could

[38]

tow several gliders, each carrying many fully armed men.

It seemed odd to be listening to an enemy pilot discuss aeronautics. If we had met in the air we would be shooting at each other.

The talk turned to a comparison between British and German fighter planes. Captain T. was frank to admit the Spitfire was as fast, if not faster, than the Messerschmitt 109. He said that the Hawker Hurricane, while a few miles per hour slower than the Me. 109, was more maneuverable. He had a healthy respect for British fighter planes. And well he might, for one of them shot him down. He mentioned the Heinkel 113, a new Nazi fighter, smaller than any other pursuit plane, but heavily gunned and very fast. This aircraft had not made its appearance over England yet, so far as I could learn.

The train slowed several times to ten miles an hour. The tommies said we were passing through areas that had had an alert, which meant enemy aircraft had been sighted in the vicinity. By traveling slowly, the train left only a small smoke trail, nearly invisible from the air. If a bomb did hit the tracks ahead, the train could stop almost immediately.

Captain T. returned to the subject of the Versailles Treaty, bitterly attacking it as the cause of the war.

One of us argued that it was the first peace treaty in history that gave the vanquished a break. We quickly discovered you can't discuss things with Nazis. They have a fanatical outlook on everything concerning the philosophy of their country, a fanaticism that defies reasoning.

"That terrible treaty," the captain roared, "never gave Germany a chance. Ach, if I escape, I will go back and climb right into a Messerschmitt."

Now that we were off the subject of aeronautics, conversation lagged. Pete brought a light back into the glum face of the German when he started talking in German. Pete had studied it while at college.

The captain was asked if there was much food shortage in Germany. He answered by describing how Royal Air Force bombers brought a plentiful supply of fish to the hungry population of Kiel.

British bombs must have exploded in a big school of herring in the Baltic Sea. Dead and stunned herring by the thousands floated into Kiel's harbor. Fishermen made record hauls and women and children filled their baskets along the shore, he said.

The train was nearing our destination so we said good-by to the prisoner after leaving him more cigarettes. I knew he was going to have an unhappy time of it, waiting in a concentration camp. We also knew he would have better food than we, if we had the bad luck to fall into the hands of his countrymen. And I don't like herring, least of all bombed herring.

The train stopped and we got out. An R.A.F. lorry that looked like a station wagon was waiting for us. The six of us climbed aboard while soldiers loaded our light luggage aboard a big R.A.F. truck. We took a good look at the town we were entering. A great wall surrounded it and it was full of medieval buildings. I felt as if I were living a thousand years ago. A big castle glowered over the town, which, the lorry driver said, was a busy city hundreds of years ago when the Romans occupied England. There was a cathedral too. Its ancient stained glass windows were still in place. In most English cathedrals the stained glass masterpieces had been removed and hidden safely away from bombs.

It was late in the afternoon and the sun cast slanting shadows, emphasizing the grand old stone buildings and narrow streets. It didn't seem that the city was bothering about a modern war until we spotted sandbags stacked around shop windows.

We left the city for the open country. After driving some distance, we came upon a collection of tents, barely discernible among the trees because, like the trees, they were dingy browns and greens. A few unpainted barnlike buildings were dispersed among the tents. An emergency army camp, I thought.

"There you are, sirs," piped up the driver, pulling off on a side road and passing two sentries. "——— Operational Training Unit."

We were used to seeing airfields with long asphalt runways, plainly marked so they could be seen easily from the air. Here, of course, everything was camouflaged to make them almost invisible.

The airport reminded me of the big lumber camps in the Pacific Northwest until we caught sight of a long open grassed space which must be the runway. I was just about to ask where the planes were when I spotted one near a tree. It was so well camouflaged I couldn't have seen it except for its propeller, which was spinning. I caught a glint on it from the late afternoon sun. There was another plane and another, all painted brown and gray-green. The woods were full of them, each one quite a distance from the next one. This was so that if a bomb got one, the rest would not be wrecked. It was quite a sight, airplanes in this Robin Hood setting. The aircraft were Miles Master trainers, the fastest training ships in the world, and long, slim-nosed Spitfires, the great British fighter planes. While aboard ship, we had studied pictures of British planes and thus were able to distinguish these two types.

We climbed out of the lorry and an Irish adjutant escorted us to an old brick building fitted up as an

[42]

office. A door opened and a tall, thin Britisher stood before us. We pulled our hands up in a "hi, bud" gesture. The officer responded with a snappy British salute.

I felt my face burn and out of the corner of my eye I saw Ayer's neck get as pink as a cooked shrimp. Here at our first meeting with the commander of the post we had saluted him as familiarly as if he were a lumber gang foreman.

Group Captain H. laughed. "They told me you were Americans," he said with a hearty British accent. "I'm glad to see you salute like them."

I knew I was going to like this fellow. We all shook hands. Then he gave us our first lesson in R.A.F. aeronautics, how to salute an officer!

"Bring the right hand up the long way and down the short way. Make it snappy!" He talked like an American.

After further lecturing on how an officer should act "because you fellows now are pilot officers in the Royal Air Force," Group Captain H. congratulated us for coming over and told us he would do everything he could to make life pleasant at the station. "We don't have quite all the comforts of home here," he explained, almost apologetically, "but we've arranged to have you fellows quartered in the wooden barracks. Most of us are still in tents."

I'd heard about stuffy English officers who specialized on etiquette and afternoon tea, but here was a regular guy. He escorted us around the airdrome and I got my first good look at a Miles Master, the trainer I'd heard so much about. Group Captain H. showed us the plane's one machine gun "to use if a Jerry gets familiar," adding that most of our shooting for a few weeks would be with a motion picture camera, fixed in the plane. When the trigger is pressed, the camera starts grinding. If your sights are on the target when you shoot, the camera will register your bull's-eyes.

I told the group captain the Master looked like a "powerful ship."

"Kennerly," he answered, "for centuries the British have been seamen. To us a ship is still a ship. Most of us wouldn't know what you meant if you called an aircraft a ship."

The Master, made entirely of plywood, was a sleek 715-horsepower two-seater with an inverted gull wing. Its top speed was 264 miles an hour. It was, of course, a lot hotter than anything I had flown and I was anxious to try her out. "If you can handle one of these," said the group captain, "you can take care of yourself in a Hurricane or Spitfire."

While we admired the aircraft, two pilots walked up and introduced themselves as Americans. They were Philip Howard Leckrone of Salem, Illinois, who was to leave soon to join a British fighter squadron, and Luke Allen, a slim, quiet fellow, who, I learned later, was an excellent flyer. It's a small world, Luke and I discovered. We'd been neighbors back in Pasadena when he was studying aeronautics at the Curtiss-Wright Institute in nearby Glendale. These fellows had been at the station a week. It looked as if there would be quite a colony of Americans among the 200 fighter pilot students at the station.

As Group Captain H. led us to a machine-gun emplacement to try our hand at target shooting, two British pilots walked past. I overheard one of them remark, "Not a bad looking bunch of blokes."

I turned around quickly and the group captain took hold of my arm. "Not so fast," he said. " 'Bloke' means the same as the American word 'guy'."

I was having a tough time learning the English language.

We practiced firing a stationary machine gun at a bull's-eye set in sand. As I held the triggers and felt the jar, I hoped it wouldn't be long before I was in the sky, firing at a swastika target.

Chapter IV

LEARNING THE TRADE

THE third day at the post we wore our new uniforms to the officers' mess for the first time. They were Royal Air Force blue. I felt like a group captain and was kidded about suddenly assuming a ramrod posture. Walking around in "civvies," as we had been doing, made us feel completely out of place at this station.

We also wore small identity tags of fireproof composition fiber. These tags, strung on stout cord which we wore around our necks, had our names and ranks stamped on them so that if we became prisoners the tags would identify us as officers and we would be treated as such. Under an international agreement, officers taken prisoners are given the same food and quality of living quarters as officers of similar rank in the nation that captures them. And while they are prisoners, the officers are paid by the captors the same salary they received while in active service in their own country.

We were finishing dinner about 5:30 P.M.—it was still broad daylight—when a siren wailed mournfully. I had heard a siren in London and knew it signaled an air raid. Some eighty of us jumped up and raced outside of the big tent which was the temporary mess.

Scanning the sky, I saw nothing. But I heard the sound of airplane motors. It was a snarly, high whine, nothing like the roar of Spitfires or Masters. Wing Commander P. and two pilots raced for a section (three) of Spitfires at the edge of the trees. Then I spotted a big two-motored monoplane about 2,000 feet up and coming toward us from the northwest. It was making a shallow dive for the field. Someone yelled, "Heinkel 111!"

Leveling off about 200 feet overhead, it dropped three black objects quickly. There were black crosses edged in white on the under side of the wings and a swastika on the tail. Immediately there were three terrific explosions on the grass runway and debris and smoke shot high into the air. The concussion blew several tents over as the Heinkel roared away.

Banking sharply just above the tree tops, it came back and headed for us. I thought it was just a show

to intimidate us. Only 100 feet from the ground, it
headed straight for me. Puffs of dust shot up around
us and there was a plunking sound as bullets whipped
into the ground. I could scarcely realize we were
being shot at. It was the first time anyone had tried
to kill me!

There was a three-foot deep ditch along the edge
of the field. We all scrambled for it and plunged in.
I jumped in feet first and fell into something soft.
Mud! I tried to keep my new uniform from getting
covered with it, but it was no use. My feet slid from
under me and I wallowed as I fell backwards, cursing Jerry.

I found myself sitting in the stuff and peering out
to see what was happening. The bomber was climbing away fast, and three Spitfires were roaring down
the debris-laden runway. They took off in tight formation and rocketed up toward the bomber. The
bomber disappeared in a cloud bank and we thought
he'd made his getaway.

Naturally everyone was excited—and mad. It was
a sight to see a long line of mud rise out of the ditch
and assume the forms of angry men.

We looked skyward. Two Spitfires were circling
under the clouds. The third one must have gone on
up. Suddenly a big aircraft emerged from the under

side of the cloud in a steep dive. It was the Heinkel! Several of us raced for three R.A.F. lorries, jumped in and roared down a road. One pilot said he knew just about where the plane would land.

I don't think I ever had a wilder ride in a plane than in that car, and I didn't have a Sutton harness to strap me down. It's a wonder we all stayed aboard. We passed several very green pastures and small houses. Just over a hill a thin column of black smoke was rising. We headed for it.

With our tires screaming as we skidded around a turn into a pasture, I saw the huge bulk of a bomber not fifty feet from a small stone house. We bounced over the rough pasture and stopped within 100 feet of the aircraft. It had been belly-landed with the undercarriage retracted and one wing was touching the ground. Smoke was coming from the cabin.

I grabbed a fire extinguisher and ran to the all-metal plane. It looked as if we could put the fire out and we began squirting extinguishers through the open door. Two of us wrapped handkerchiefs over our noses and crawled inside. We worked our way to the nose where we found extinguishers and began using them. Other fellows shoveled dirt on the flames. Soon the fire was out. The British wanted to save the bomber so they could study it.

The fact that oil had been spilled in the cabin indicated the Nazis had set the blaze. They couldn't have gotten very far, if they had tried to escape.

Some of the boys who had gone into the house came out and invited us to "come in and meet some flyers." We hurried in. The living room presented a strange sight. Several of our pilots were there, plus a little old woman and four German flyers.

One Nazi was stepping out of his heavy flying suit. His uniform, of course, was underneath. Two others were seated at a table, drinking tea from dainty cups. The fourth was stretched out on a couch and the woman was bandaging his arm.

The woman, who must have been seventy at least, had heard the crash and gone out to see what had happened. When she saw three Germans crawl from the bomber, carrying the fourth one, she had invited them in for tea.

"I don't have a gun," she said brightly, "so that was the only way I could keep them here until the soldiers arrived."

One of the Germans was pouting. He wouldn't look up or speak. But the fellow who had just removed his flying suit seemed quite amused at his hostess. He spoke English and talked freely.

He let us examine his flying suit and we found it

to be all-leather, lined with the finest sheepskin. It was electrically heated. Wires, as in a heating pad, were woven through it and all the wearer had to do was plug a wire from the suit into a socket in the plane. The pilot's suit was equipped with a "throat mike." This radio microphone consists of two little pads pressed lightly against the throat. Its chief advantage over the ordinary mike is that it doesn't pick up the noise of your engine or other sounds in the aircraft.

The pilot explained the workings of the life belt he and his crew wore. It consisted of a pair of straps crossing over the shoulders and chest and hooking onto a belt. It resembled the bosomy English "Mae West" life jacket except that it wasn't worn inflated. Consequently it wasn't as bulky. As soon as a man wearing the Nazi outfit hit the water, he pulled a wire attached to a metal cylinder about the size of a twelve-gauge shotgun shell. Filled with highly compressed air, it was attached to his life belt. As soon as the wire was pulled, the cylinder released the air and it immediately inflated the life jacket.

Soldiers took the prisoners away. We returned to the Heinkel and removed one of the front machine guns. We also pried the rivets loose on one wing to remove a panel on which was painted a black cross.

From the groove along the ground made by the bomber in the belly-landing, we knew the pilot was a good one. When you have to land an aircraft in a short space, the only way to bring her down is with wheels up. The whole belly acts as a brake and you don't travel far before you stop.

Returning to the airdrome with the booty, we congratulated Wing Commander P., who had brought the Jerry down. We asked him how he scored the victory.

He said that while his two pilots stayed below the clouds to tackle the Jerry if he came down, he flew above and waited.

"I circled around a bit, hoping Jerry would come on up. I was about 1,000 feet above the cloud when the Heinkel came through. I made a dive immediately and got close enough astern of the bomber so I could see the rear gunners training their guns over the Heinkel's tail, thinking that any aircraft following would come up behind them.

"Not one of the crew saw me. I got a long burst at the pilot. The aircraft rolled over, went out of control and went down in an inverted spin. I followed it into the cloud and lost it."

This incident occurred just after Hitler opened the second phase of his aerial war against Britain.

[52]

The first phase, which began after the Dunkirk evacuation at the end of May and continued until mid-August, was a concentration of aerial fury on British shipping in the English Channel. The R.A.F. had been so successful countering this that the Luftwaffe turned its attention in trying, unsuccessfully, to destroy the R.A.F. ground bases. The so-called first phase having failed, Hitler dubbed this the second phase of the battle for Britain.

The next morning I made my first flight in a Miles Master. A British pilot sat in the rear cockpit and I was in the front. What a digout that Kestrel motor gave her! She was off the ground almost as soon as she took the throttle. Once in the air I immediately lost sight of the airdrome. It blended into the countryside of rolling hills, canals, and villages.

The Britisher must have noticed my perplexity through his rear-view mirror, because he laughed. I could hear him through the earphones. We both wore headphones and were equipped with speaking tubes.

"Nice bit of camouflaging, eh?" he said. I nodded and continued to stare like a blind man. I wanted to know where we were in case he told me to take over and bring her in.

He banked around and dropped for what appeared to be a meadow. As we approached to within 150 feet of the ground, I picked out some buildings and a couple of aircraft on the grass runway. We made a perfect landing and the Britisher held his hands over his head and ordered, "Take her over, Kennerly."

I'd held the dual control stick while he flew so I'd get the feel of the plane. It was plenty hot on the controls. At the down-wind end of the runway I pressed right rudder, squeezed the brake handle and gave her a little throttle to turn her around. Next thing I knew we had spun a complete circle and almost tipped her over on a wing.

"Steady, steady!" came through the earphones. The controls were jerked away. "You're not driving a truck."

I suddenly decided this was a very sensitive and powerful aircraft. The slight throttle I had given her was too much and I had over-controlled on the rudder. The Britisher straightened her out and waved his arms for me to take over. He seemed more confident of my skill than I was.

I taxied to the take-off and turned around all right. We got a green light and I opened the throttle wide. Immediately the tail rose from the ground. We barely seemed to have started when she took off by herself! I thought surely we were going to crash because we didn't have flying speed.

"Kennerly," came the instructions, "hold more right rudder. You're not correcting enough for torque."

I made a careful circle on instruments, calculated to bring us back to where we had taken off. This way I thought I could find the 'drome. I kept my eyes on it. I eased off the throttle and began descending into the wind. The wail of a horn sounded, as if we were being followed by one of those absurd miniature English cars. At the same time a red light appeared on the dashboard. This was the automatic warning that the undercarriage was retracted. It went into action when the throttle was cut and the landing wheels still were up.

I pushed the lever which lowered the wheels and the horn stopped. After all this confusion I still had enough presence of mind to drop the flaps. We came in awfully close to the tree tops and I gave her a little throttle. We passed the last trees and I aimed her for the green grass.

On the left edge of the runway was a Master turned cross-wind. Instead of remaining there, it began rolling across in front of us just as our wheels touched the turf. The plane was but twenty feet away. Automatically I kicked left rudder. We skidded sideways, a sickening skid that brought my heart up in my throat. Our nose went down and the tail rose high over our heads. I thought we were going on over. I opened the throttle wide and the spinning prop' bit into the three-inch long grass and shot a shower of green high in the air.

By yanking the stick back, the propeller blasted the tail down and we bumped and rolled to a stop in front of a group of student pilots, who were scattering away in all directions.

"Taxi over to that aircraft!" ordered the pilot. We coasted over and the officer "tore a strip" off two student pilots in the plane. "Tearing a strip" is R.A.F. for giving them hell. I was a little shaky for awhile until my instructor told me he and I were working the controls during the emergency and our actions jibed so perfectly neither of us realized at the time what the other was doing. The "sky prof" had watched me follow through on the controls.

So much for the first hop. There were many more, although fortunately none like that one. We flew in all kinds of weather. And I never saw such fog! It got so thick at times that even the sea gulls had to carry maps to find their way about. It forced us to become experts at blind flying. Along with the flight work, we went through an intensive ground school. We learned the Morse code, each interceptor being equipped with a Morse key as well as a microphone. We studied navigation, including how to plot a course by compass or by stars. We learned considerable meteorology and found out how to detect air thermals and down-drafts.

We studied radio transmission, or R.T. procedure, which included how to keep in touch with the radio controller on the ground so he could follow on a map the progress of our flight and could direct us to the enemy. We practiced singing in a high voice the R.T. responses. Although this sounded like blazes to us while we were vocalizing, over the R.T. it sounded much clearer and more incisive than when we talked in normal tones.

We practiced in the air giving and receiving battle signals, such as firing the colors of the day from the Very pistols in the cockpit, and receiving from the ground the response of the letters of the day, flashed to us from an Aldis lamp. These signals are used at night when you approach a British airdrome to land and the insignia on your wings can't be seen. If the 'drome challenges you with the colors of the day, you give them in Morse code the letters of the day. These are flashed from an amber light under the tail assembly. If the 'drome winks the letters of the day, you respond with the colors of the day by firing the Very pistol in the cockpit. These letters and colors are changed often so Jerry won't become familiar with them.

We took machine guns apart and put them together. We loaded and unloaded the air-cooled guns, mounted in wings of fighter planes. Each fighter pilot has a crew of eight men to take care of his ship, including keeping her supplied with ammunition, but you never can tell when your aircraft will be forced down and you will have to do some quick reloading yourself.

We were put through the ropes of blind flying, both in a Link Trainer and "under the hood" in the Master.

As for training in the air, hour after hour, we took turns acting as safety pilot for each other while one of us flew "under the hood" entirely on instruments. We made practice dive attacks on white cloth box kites towed by Fairey Battles, light British bombers. We fired on the kites with cameras and machine guns.

It was a glorious, realistic training. It was thrilling to feel ourselves growing more sure at the controls, more precise in our maneuvers, more accurate in our marksmanship. Some of us secretly wanted to meet a Nazi with our one lone machine gun. We thought we could bring him down and show the old timers, who used eight machine guns, that it could be done. It's a good thing we didn't meet one!

There were thrills in the training, even though no Nazi bomber came over to play target for us. One sunny afternoon I was safety pilot while Luke was getting a little "under the hood" practice. He had made a fine take-off, completely on instruments and we had climbed perhaps 100 feet. It was a cold, late autumn day and the hatch had been pushed up, providing a windscreen for me but leaving the sides and rear open so a breeze could come in. The movable seat was raised to increase visibility.

Without thinking, I pulled down the hatch. I'd forgotten to lower the seat and the hatch slammed shut, conking me on the head, stunning me, and shoving my head forward and down. I was too jammed together to speak through the tube to Luke. If he got in trouble, he'd never know it, for, of course, his cockpit was covered by a black hood.

I was woozy for a moment, then struggled to free myself from the pressure that was shutting off my wind. It was no use. I just jammed myself in tighter. I felt the aircraft making a couple of steep banks and wondered if we were far enough from the ground to turn safely. I strained neck muscles trying to force my head into a position where I could look at the

[59]

instrument panel but I grew dizzy instead. I raised a hand and waved it as high as I could. Then I realized Luke couldn't see it. It was an unhealthy situation. There were many aircraft in the sky and Luke was relying on me to warn him or take over the controls if we got in a tight spot.

The pain in my neck was terrific. I wriggled my right arm back and below, grasping for a lever. I felt one and hoped it wasn't the flap controls. Moving it, I felt the pressure on my neck diminish. It was the lever that lowered the seat. I sat up and stretched. What a relief! We were skimming along just above a cloud bank. The altimeter read 7,000 feet and our speed 210 miles an hour. Looking at the rear cockpit the faithful pilot was still under the hood. Through the tube I told him what had happened. He just laughed and said, "That proves I can fly better under the hood than you can with full visibility!" Unsympathetic rat! He didn't even bother to come out from his hood.

Far off to starboard I spotted another plane. Taking over the controls, I steered for it. I could almost see the Nazi crosses on the wings, that is until I identified it as another Master. We sped toward each other. Flying by himself was one of the American pilots.

He held aloft a map and shook his head, indicating he had lost his way. This was the guy who bragged about his navigation ability. He used to say that finding your way in an English fog is a cinch. "All you have to do is dive close to the ground, pick out a landmark and pin-point yerself." He seemed to have undaunted faith in this pin-pointing, for we often found him booming around in the sky by himself, a map spread across his knees. When he spotted another plane, however, he invariably would make for it and signal that he had lost his bearings.

I motioned to him to follow us. He seemed glad to tag along, for he fell in, line astern, just below our tail-wheel. He stuck close, not wanting us to shake him off.

Finally Luke came out of his aerial cave to see what was going on. I pointed to our rear guard and Luke laughed through the speaking tube: "We gotta play pin-point again."

After my recent near strangulation, I had no idea where we were so I motioned Luke to take her down. When Luke made a maneuver in an aircraft, it was a snappy one. Down we went, almost losing our pal as we dipped steeply into the wet whiteness of the clouds.

We darted from under the cloud to see, stretching away to dim indistinctness, the snaky line of the

Welsh coast. Just off shore were some tiny dots, pleasure boats. I caught Luke's eye. He nodded and took us down in a joyful, roaring dive, straight for the boats. Luke aimed for one boat. The noise of our motors must have been tearing at the eardrums of the boats' occupants.

Down we streaked. Luke eased off on the throttle and just when it seemed the nose of our aircraft would smash into the lead boat, he hauled back on the stick and gunned her again.

We missed the boat's mast by twenty feet and boomed upwards. Both of us looked back to see the propeller wash send up sweeps of spray over the boats. One ship nearly capsized when the prop' blast caught the sail, bellied it out instantly and tilted the ship far over.

No sooner had the fishermen recovered from our dive than the second Master gave them the other barrel. It's a tough life for a seaman when there are playful pilots in the vicinity.

We circled, threatening them with another dive and then roared down toward the beach. We dusted it off a few times, sending up explosive clouds of sand as we dipped to within six feet of the ground.

A gang of fishermen who were spreading their nets on the sand shook their fists at us. We came back at them, forcing them to flatten themselves on the beach. Good thing we didn't have to make an emergency landing there. Finally we'd had about enough, so we headed for home.

One flight I never will forget was in a Fairey Battle, a two-place bomber, used extensively for training. A pilot took eight of us aboard the thing. He was taking us to a nearby airdrome to see a Spitfire put through its paces by Pilot H., a sandy-headed little guy, who could make an airplane do everything but play a piano.

The eight of us managed to squeeze into the belly of the single-engined bomber. The pilot took his place calmly at the controls. I wondered just how the 1,035-horsepower motor, the same size as used in some single-seated Hurricanes, could lift nine men into the air.

After practically running off the end of the field, the aircraft clumsily lifted itself. I was sure we couldn't clear the trees beyond the field. But we did. It was an unusual experience, packed in the belly of this bomber. We landed in a short time and one by one we clambered out. As I reached the sunlight, three high Royal Air Force officers were staring with unbelieving eyes.

"I say, old chap," one of them was saying to the

pilot, "don't you think it a bit risky, turning a Fairey Battle into a Lisbon Clipper?"

Hundreds of flyers and student pilots lined the landing strip of this big airdrome. It was like circus day at home, except that everybody in this crowd wore a uniform. We met H., who said he hoped to show us some flying we had never seen in our own country. He got into a sleek new Spitfire and roared off.

Circling a couple of times until he reached about 2,000 feet—he got up there in no time at all—he came down in a dive. And a Spitfire in a dive is a sight and sound to remember. Instead of pulling out of the dive normally, he made an outside loop. If his Sutton harness had given way, he would have shot from his cockpit like a bullet. As he dusted off the ground at the base of his loop, we cheered. Then he shot into the sky as if catapulted from a gigantic sling. I never saw so fast a plane. He circled, bringing her around so quickly he must have blacked out. Next we knew he was fifty feet off the ground, doing slow rolls at 250 miles an hour. Then he was up to about 1,500 feet, dropping into a spin and coming out of it quickly and precisely. After a few more maneuvers he landed and the show was over.

We thought we were pretty good pilots until we

saw this demonstration. Perhaps that was why we had been brought down here.

Going home, four of the boys had to ride in a car. The other five of us took off, including the pilot, who must have been feeling his aeronautical oats after watching the Spitfire. He spotted an army camp on the way back and he took us down in a dive. We wore no safety belts and had to hang onto the airplane's metal ribs to keep from being tossed around. We dove over the tops of the square tents and zoomed up. The propeller blast collapsed one tent and sent its occupants streaming wild-eyed from under the flapping canvas. Pegs were pulled up from other tents. Next we flew over some marshy country and made steep-banked turns fifteen feet off the ground. I swore time and again we were going to dig a wing into the muck. Finally we got safely home.

There were more weeks of heavy training—aerobatics, formation flying, gunnery. Several of the boys got nosebleeds from aerobatics. We had some real headaches, too, after power dives of several thousand feet, when our ears popped like firecrackers. The ability to fly formation was stressed. Aircraft fly close together during maneuvers in England so as not to lose each other in the fog. In a section of three, the two rear aircraft's wings are about six feet back and

[65]

inside the trailing edge of the leader's wings. The three planes fly on the same level. In America the rear planes fly a little above the leader.

More Americans arrived at the post. Stanley Kolendorski, a Polish-American, came from Lakehurst, New Jersey. Then there was Gregory Daymond, another southern Californian, who hailed from Van Nuys. This slim handsome pilot was only nineteen. Other arrivals were Edwin ("Bud") Orbison and Dean Satterlee, both from Sacramento, California. The American colony had grown to eleven, six of us from California. Luke might have made it seven from California, for he had lived there, but his registered home state was New Mexico. I don't know why there were so many of us from the same state, unless it was that flying has been unusually popular in California since John J. Montgomery made his first glider flight near San Diego in 1884. That 600-foot hop, by the way, was the first flight made in the United States.

We Americans were "attacked" one day by thirty-one British newspapermen and newsreel boys, who descended en masse on us from London. We put on quite a show for them, taking them for rides in the Masters and making formation flights for the cameras. Shortly afterwards we made a recording at the airdrome for the B.B.C., which was broadcast to America. We described our life in England and had the opportunity to tell the world what a great training school we were attending.

It's a good thing the radio announcer didn't ask Kolendorski what he thought of English stoves. It was just a couple of days before the recording was made that I noticed black smoke sifting from the door of Kolendorski's room. I hurried to it and squinted in. Seated on his bed writing a letter and nearly obliterated in smoke was the flyer, a gas mask covering his swarthy face!

As I started to laugh, he jumped up and came tearing out, emitting smothered, profane yells for his batman. The batman finally fixed the offending iron stove which was causing the trouble, explaining that the wind outside was so strong, it was blowing the smoke back down the four-inch pipe. When the atmosphere cleared, Kolendorski resumed his writing, but left his mask on as a precaution.

Chapter V

AUTUMN TINTS—NAZI STYLE

IN MID-SEPTEMBER Luke and I got our first full week's leave. We wanted a look at this brave little country we were going to fight for and decided to start with Liverpool, England's third largest city.

Arriving there a little past noon, we were strolling not far from the sweep of docks by the Mersey Estuary, when a low wail spread over the city. An air raid alarm! The well-filled streets began to empty as wardens blew whistles and directed people to shelters. Many persons continued unconcernedly on their various ways. Busses, automobiles and taxis kept moving.

Barrage balloons hung motionless overhead. They were up several thousand feet. Luke pointed east. About 7,000 feet above the balloons and traveling very fast were five gray bombers. From their twin motors, extending forward from the wings and even

[68]

with the nose, we recognized them as Junkers 88's. These were Germany's fast bombers that had set records for speed and carrying capacity.

The "whap! whap!" of antiaircraft began. Black puffs in clusters of three and four broke around the big craft. Unconcernedly the bombers came on, still in formation. They were after the docks, one of Britain's lifelines. The ground shook and we heard a heavy "garumph!" A black smoke blotch fanned skyward a couple of blocks away. That was the first one.

There were two more explosions. Streaks of debris and fire shot aloft with the smoke. The bombs were hitting the business district, but not the docks. Several geysers spouted harmlessly in the Mersey. The balloons and flak were keeping the bombers too high to aim with any accuracy.

As we stood, cursing the Jerries and wishing we were aloft to tackle them even in our light Miles Masters, two sections of fighters swarmed up swiftly to meet the bombers. Their elliptical wings revealed they were Spitfires. We egged them on, as did many others who had stopped to watch the show.

Never losing formation, the bombers wheeled and streaked eastward, the Spitfires climbing rapidly in hot pursuit. Later we heard the Spitfires caught the

88's and knocked down one of them over England and accounted for three more over the Channel. An expensive raid for the Huns!

Sirens shrieked down a side street and an ambulance passed us. We ran after it and rounded a corner to see a crowd gathering in front of what appeared to be a department store. The crowd arched into the street to make way for rescue workers and ambulances.

Elbowing through the throng we saw a gaping hole gashed through the sidewalk and part of the street. Someone said nearly a hundred people had been trapped in the store basement. A bomb had shot through the street and exploded in the basement.

Other than the probing rescue crews, there was no sign of a human being in the tumbled wreckage. The rescuers were covered with a pulverized dust which was finer than face powder. The force of high explosive bombs is so terrific it pulverizes concrete and rocks, shattering them into the softest kind of dust.

Seeing there was nothing we could do to aid the trained A.R.P. crews, we left shortly.

Next afternoon we arrived in London. Not so many months before, probably the world's capital of commerce, now a vast, grim fortress, London that September afternoon was resolute. Tank traps in her historic streets and machine-guns peeping from her ancient buildings served notice that she was ready to defend herself. Instead of being decorated with ancient cannon which in times past had boomed forth British victories, the parks were emplacements for long-nosed, sleek antiaircraft guns, all pointed skyward. I was proud to belong to the armed forces of a nation that was willing to accept battle in her own back yard.

While another section of the city was undergoing a raid, we visited St. Paul's Cathedral. As we walked up Ludgate Hill and saw this magnificent church, it seemed to symbolize the eternal strength of Britain. The most striking thing to me about England was the antiquity of things, the history and tradition surrounding them. On this hill, back in the days of the Caesars, there was supposed to have been a Roman temple. That was hundreds and hundreds of years ago! Where I came from a fifty-year-old building is venerable.

St. Paul's, with its huge dome, dominated the city. From this vantage point we could see streaks of smoke to the east. Fires started the night before by the Nazis still were being extinguished. It was at the beginning of the all-out raids on the city.

Inside St. Paul's we admired the busts and tributes

to England's great fighting men. Heretofore history, to me, had been a list of dates in a schoolbook. Here was much of England's history enshrined. We saw the bust of George Washington, beside which was soon to be placed a memorial plaque that would read: "Pilot Officer William Mead Lindsley Fiske III, Royal Air Force. An American citizen who died that England might live. August 18, 1940." He was the first American pilot killed in the war.

We'd heard about the big air raid shelters of London and wanted to see some of them. Hailing a taxi we told the driver to go to the East End, the intensely bombed, poorer section.

Twice we detoured roped-off streets where men, bull-dozers and small steam shovels were clearing debris. There were a few "vacant lots" between buildings and some buildings showed scars. Afternoon shadows were beginning to lengthen and the streets still were fairly well crowded. We saw no planes overhead, although we occasionally heard distant gunfire.

Arriving at the East End, we didn't have to be told it probably was the hardest hit section of London. One entire block was a leveled mass of ashes with an occasional blackened chimney jutting futilely into the sky. The driver parked near a short line of people and said, "this is it, sir." After telling him to wait, we skirted the queue and were admitted into a doorway that looked like others along the block except that the door was open. It was the entrance to a shelter. Seeing our uniforms, a man who introduced himself as an assistant warden of the shelter, offered to show us the place. We thanked him and, of course, accepted.

He led us down a flight of damp stairs past a small cubbyhole of an office. Near it was a first aid station. Our guide said that people already were coming in to take their places for the night, adding, "We are doing away with long lines of people standing at the entrance, waiting to get in, by giving them numbers and assigning them to specific shelters."

Along one side of the vast cellar, dim lights revealed rows of wagons. In them several people already were asleep, their feet and arms sticking grotesquely over the sides of the wagons. One elderly woman, wrapped in a blanket and seated on a folding camp chair, unconcernedly was fixing her nails. All the people looked poor.

"How many people sleep here?" I asked.

"Eight thousand," the warden answered.

How so many people crammed into so small a space and didn't suffocate was beyond me!

The warden explained that when no raids were on during the day, the women and children returned to their homes, if they still had them, otherwise they were cared for at government camps. The men, of course, went to work during the day. The government provided pensions for all civilians injured by the war, as well as for war widows and orphans. In addition, the people were compensated for all damage done to their property.

We walked blocks, it seemed. Finally we came to a place where men were setting up three-tiered bunks. Heavy burlap had been nailed to them to sleep on. The top bunk was about six feet off the ground. Each bed bore a number. "This is the way we hope we have them all fixed," the warden explained. We asked him if all the people slept either in bunks or wagons. He laughed and answered that most of them slept on the floor. Some slept on carpets, others merely in their clothes or blankets.

About this time Luke and I agreed we'd seen enough. People were crowding in and hunting for their "accommodations."

Our taxi driver was waiting for us. We told him to take us to the subways, which had been converted to shelters.

We arrived at a subway entrance and found it, too,

thronged with people. They were better dressed than those we had just seen, and flocked into the subway as calmly as if they were returning home from a late afternoon shopping tour. The adaptability of these Britishers to this cave man existence was a marvel to me. I wondered how many of us who flew and who loved "wide open spaces" could have stood this way of living.

Luke and I followed the crowd down the longest escalator I had ever seen. We must have descended sixty feet. The escalator was not operating, for it was used to sleep on at night. In contrast to the East End shelter, this one was brightly lighted. Being sixty feet below ground, it was one of the safest in London. Even though the people had hardly begun to pack themselves together in sardine-like rows along the subway platform, the air was unpleasantly close. A uniformed warden we questioned about ventilation said the only things that brought in fresh air were the subway trains as they passed by in the night. He said the trains didn't disturb in the least the tired sleepers, many of whom lay only inches away from the train tracks.

For awhile we watched the crowd coming into the brightly lighted subterranean station. Families arranged themselves along the walls and discussed the

[75]

affairs of the day. Children had their hair combed and then were tucked with blankets or coats into their "beds" on the floor. People began crowding in fast now. Someone said a raid had started. There was not the slightest evidence of panic or distress. Someone remarked, "Why in blazes did those dirty Germans have to start so early tonight?" I felt that, as a pilot, I had a lot to learn from these sturdy people.

The first time the human stream down the escalator slacked off, Luke and I picked our way upstairs. We reached the top and luxuriously filled our lungs with fresh air. It was growing dusk. There was a rumble of guns somewhere not far off. We heard another rumble, a heavy, surging drone—Nazi bombers far overhead. The recurring surge was caused by the motors being desynchronized. This was done to confuse the British plane detectors. It is difficult to tell, if bombers desynchronize their motors, the number of aircraft in a formation. We also recognized the roar of night-fighting British Defiants and Hurricanes.

The sky was getting too dark to see planes, particularly as high as the Germans must be flying. From the heaviness of the sound there must have been many of them.

Luke thought our shelter tour incomplete without

a squint at the ritzy Savoy Hotel bar, said to be absolutely bomb-proof. We taxied to the hotel and entered the swanky subterranean cocktail lounge. The place was full of smartly dressed people. Several wore long faces, quite a contrast to the universal cheerfulness we'd seen in other shelters. After a drink I suggested we leave. Luke nodded and we pulled out.

The ground shook as a bomb exploded near by. Things were warming up! Despite this, many people still were abroad, most of them in uniform. A taxicab shot by us pulling a fire truck trailer loaded with hose. Riding the running board and clinging to the careening cab were three firemen. Evidently they had commandeered the cab and attached to it one of London's hundreds of truck trailers.

We ran in the direction the cab had taken. An orange light haloed the skyline to our left. That meant the Jerries already had begun dumping incendiary bombs. The blast of antiaircraft was almost continuous, punctuated frequently by heavy muffled explosions of bombs. Searchlight beams lined the sky. We watched seven of them weave back and forth and finally converge on one point. In the hub of the cross fire of beams was a Nazi plane. Pin-points of light broke out around it. Antiaircraft shells. The plane began twisting and diving, trying to evade the lights. But two or three beams managed to stick with it. Although the bomber was painted black to escape detection, it made a bright spot when the lights hit it. Like a wild animal caught in a trap, the Jerry writhed, trying to break away into protecting darkness. The chase was fascinating to watch. I often admired the accuracy of the antiaircraft gunners, but never had occasion before to appreciate the marksmanship of the men behind the searchlights. It must be a real job, swinging those heavy lights to keep their long beams concentrated on a target moving as fast as an airplane.

Suddenly there was a bright flash where the bomber had been. A shower of sparks fell from the spot. That was the last we saw of him.

There was a continuous racket now. Bombs were exploding frequently and archies were hurling steady barrages of deadly missiles high in the air. The glow, increasing in brightness over the tops of the buildings, disclosed that people on the streets were not running to shelter and showed no signs of panic. I guess it was this atmosphere of calmness that helped keep us from feeling apprehensive. It was contagious.

As we started toward the fire, the crowd thinned out. We passed several doorways which had dim blue lights over the portals, marking entrances to shelters. Occasionally we passed a fire spotter silhouetted on a roof top against the ruddy sky. There must be a whale of a fire not far from us. Red cinders began falling. We had to keep brushing our coats to keep the cinders from burning them.

More fire apparatus flashed by. As we reached an intersection, a cab, with little slits of headlights crawled by. There was too much noise for the driver to hear us hail him so we ran to the cab, telling him to take us to the fire. We realized the Nazi bombers would be attracted to the blaze as moths to a flame. Their night raid technique, of course, was to send their ace pilots and bombadiers over at dusk to pick out the objectives and drop thousands of incendiaries on them so the other bomber formations could use the resulting fires as guides. The Nazis weren't particular about picking military objectives over London. They were just trying unsuccessfully to carry out Hitler's boast that he could blast London off the map with fire and dynamite.

The driver drove slowly, not knowing when a fire engine might shoot across his path. Suddenly ahead of us on the street surface an ugly red ball of fire appeared in the darkness. It began spewing like a cutting torch and the redness turned to white. An incendiary bomb! It was beginning to eat right through the street.

We stopped as several dim figures hurried toward it, one of them carried a bucket. Another fire appeared on the sidewalk near a building. Then another. A marquee half a block ahead began burning.

The driver asked us if we wanted to go any farther. "If you can get around these people, go," I urged. One man advanced on the molten mass in the street. It was blindingly bright to look at. He appeared to be carrying a small shield ahead of him. The white light dimmed and went out as he smothered it with sand. A plane can carry from 1,000 to 2,000 small incendiary bombs, which when scattered over an area of several blocks, start scores of fires. The firemen wanted to keep all blazes extinguished on this street, no doubt, to keep it open for fire apparatus.

At the next intersection, the street was covered with water. Mains had burst ahead of us. If enough mains were hit, the water pressure would go down, seriously hampering fire-fighting operations.

Down a side street, it seemed more brightly illuminated than by sunlight, a double-decked bus lumbered along. Except for the driver, it appeared to be empty.

As we watched the bus, a great light flashed directly under it. There was a jarring explosion. It was jerked bodily off the street and hurled upward and into the face of a four-story building! The driver rolled out of a bus window and fell onto the street. From the same explosion, the front of the building was sliding down into the street. The bus landed upright on heavy timbers which projected from the now frontless building, like handles on a wheelbarrow. The timbers were about eight feet above the sidewalk and there was the bus, parked high overhead.

Our taxi driver pulled over to the curb and stopped. We paid him quickly and ran down the street toward the bus. Cinders were falling fast, but we didn't stop to brush them off. Now we could see the flames of a huge fire that was less than a block away from the bus, although fortunately on the other side of the street.

We slopped through water which covered the sidewalk. On the dry side of the street a blue flame shot high in the air. We could hear it roar above the din. It was gas burning from a ruptured main. My eyeballs burned and it was difficult to breathe. There wasn't much smoke but the heat was very intense. It was getting windy as the great fire, which was consuming buildings a block away and eating into those across the street, created its own draft. The

[81]

flames made a solid roar which muffled gunfire and exploding bombs. Four big extension ladder trucks were parked about 200 yards down the street, firemen atop the ladders playing streams into the inferno.

When we reached him, the bus driver was sitting up, his head hanging forward. He was shaking it slowly. Blood was coming from his mouth. We brushed live sparks from his hair and clothes then carried him as gently as we could to the shelter of a doorway. He looked at us gratefully through blood-shot eyes, but didn't speak. I felt carefully for broken bones but could find none. Luke crawled up on the timbers to have a look into the bus, which was still perched grotesquely on the beams. Fortunately there had been no one else aboard.

I heard a whirring noise and at almost the same instant something smacked my steel helmet so hard my knees sagged. Instinctively I lunged farther into the protection of the doorway. Above the fire's roar I heard a zinging sound. It came from the street. Squinting against the glare I looked at the pavement. The high center arch which wasn't covered with water flashed with pin-point lights. At first I thought they were spots before my eyes from the head blow. When a chunk of black, torn metal bounced at my feet, I realized the flashes were made by shrapnel

[82]

drumming on the street and striking sparks. There was a regular hail of the stuff.

"Get under cover!" I shouted to Luke, who had refused to wear his steel helmet. All he had on his head was his R.A.F. officer's hat, no protection against this rain of steel. Luke merely grinned and pointed to what must have been a sizable dent in my hat.

The steel-helmeted firemen continued fighting the roaring fire, paying no more attention to the shrapnel than if it were a light spring shower. London had a force of 30,000 men in her fire department, 20,000 active and 10,000 in reserve. It was this gallant force, as well as the R.A.F., that saved London from becoming "scorched earth."

The heat was getting so intense I pulled out a handkerchief, slopped it in the gutter water, rinsed it out and wrapped it around my nose and mouth. Breathing became easier. I moistened the wounded man's handkerchief and after cleaning the blood from his face, put the handkerchief over it. We must get him out of here quickly. Pressure of the heat against my eyelids forced me to hold them open with my thumb in order to see.

The ground trembled with an explosion. A shower of sparks burst high in the air. There was a second

[83]

explosion in the same place and in a few seconds a third. Luke yelled that it must be a chain bomb, several bombs chained together that fall in the same small area and explode at short intervals. Luckily this one, if that's what it was, fell in the middle of a fire.

We couldn't get to the firemen a block away. A building on our side of the street was on fire and cut us off from them. We didn't want to take a chance running the gauntlet of flames with a wounded man. So we had to leave by the way we had come.

Luke and I picked up the man and stumbled along close to the buildings. He and I each kept one hand free to pry our eyes open. The man, an arm slung over each of our shoulders, had fainted.

The shrapnel was still falling pretty thick so Luke walked along closest to the buildings, which were brightly illuminated from the glaring caldron of fire across the street. I felt as though my face and side nearest the fire were being cooked. Twice we had to enter a doorway to cool off. Even then there was little relief.

It seemed an age before we reached the first cross street. Turning the corner we felt a welcome cool blast of air which was being drawn toward the fire. The three of us sat down on the curb, our feet ankle deep in gutter water. We mopped our faces with the water as well as the face of the driver. The cool water brought him to with a groan.

As I looked around to see if I could spot a truck or cab a great "whoosh" and terrific roar knocked me flat. Next thing I knew I was choking. Opening my eyes, everything before me was a foggy brown. I knew a bomb had exploded near by and that I was eating dust it had created. I sat up and heard Luke's voice. He was swearing.

The dust began to clear a little and I saw Luke climbing out of the gutter. The wounded fellow still was sitting up, his head in his hands. Then I heard the most welcome sound. It was the roaring motor of a truck! Luke must have seen it for he wobbled out in the middle of the street and began waving his arms. The truck came through the dust and stopped. Two men climbed out. They looked like men from Mars, their faces distorted by protruding eye-pieces and tubes. They were wearing masks.

I got up to go toward them. My head spun around and I fell. It was just dizziness and I took several deep breaths and got to my feet again. The dust from the bomb, which had lit in the middle of the street not eighty feet from us, still was thick. The men with masks picked up the bus driver and carried him to the cab.

[85]

Then they helped us into the empty back end of the truck and gave us a pull at a whisky bottle. It sent hot fire through me and bucked me up considerably. The truck driver said he would take the wounded man to a hospital. We asked him to drop us off at a hotel on the way.

The truck started off, leaving the fire zone. Shrapnel began falling again. A piece of it pinged on the metal bed of the truck, which had no top over the back. Luke and I were stretched out, getting our wind. We were too relaxed to crawl near the cab for shelter. My eyes still burned like live coals and it was good to open them and feel the cool night air on them.

The truck was rolling along at a good clip through sheer blackness. The driver must have had the eyes of an owl to see where he was going. Above the rumble of the truck, which evidently had been used to haul rubble, the archies still were roaring.

Finally the truck stopped. We got out and took a look at the wounded bus driver, who was able to talk hoarsely. He thanked us for picking him up, and we told him we were glad he didn't appear badly hurt. The truck driver pointed down a side street and said a hotel was only a half block away. We thanked him and started walking off in the darkness, both of us still a little weak in the knees.

[86]

We'd gone only a few steps when shrapnel began sending up pin-points of fire from the street. I suggested going into the pub at the corner and wait until things quieted a bit. I was still worried about Luke's head. But he wasn't and insisted we go on.

Suddenly a big chunk of metal swished through the plate glass window of a shop directly in front of us. Glass showered our legs. I could see Luke's surprised face. "Let's stop in at a pub for a minute," he agreed.

After a quick one at the bar we decided to take a look out. It was quiet so we hot-footed it down the street. Several store windows had been smashed, glass fragments from them littering the sidewalk. There was lots of valuable merchandise in the dark windows. We knew the stuff was safe even though unprotected because looting was almost unheard of over here. We came upon a small sign which said only: "Hotel."

We went in and engaged a room from a timid little landlady. The room was on the fifth and top floor. We'd no sooner crawled into bed than a couple of bombs dropped uncomfortably close and we could hear bits of steel hit the roof. Someone knocked on the door. In answer to a somewhat gruff, "Who's there?" a half frightened voice answered that it was the landlady and she wanted us to come down to "the comfortable shelter below the lounge."

Luke thanked her and told her he was going to sleep where he was. A little later the building shook again. After a few moments there was another knock. This time the landlady pleaded with us. I told her we paid to sleep in the room, not in the shelter and to leave us alone. We went back to sleep.

A third time we were wakened by the knock of the over-solicitous woman. Apparently things were still hot and heavy overhead. She again insisted we go to the shelter.

"Say," Luke stormed, "did you notice how red the eyeballs of my friend were?"

The woman said she did.

"He has a terrible case of pink eye. Very catching, you know. I wouldn't want it to spread among your guests."

Needless to say, we spent the rest of the night in peace!

Chapter VI

EAGLE WINGS

"This is a memorable occasion for both Britain and America!"

That final night at the station, Group Captain H. was really worked up as he spoke to us Americans in the officer's mess.

"Boys, this night takes me back to the first World War. In those brave days I trained with young American flyers who later made heroes of themselves in the Lafayette Escadrille Corps. Tonight I bid godspeed to you Americans of another generation. You are about to form your own squadron which will carry on the glory of the old Lafayette Escadrille. Good luck."

The party might have been called our "graduation exercises." Tomorrow we were leaving for a central England airdrome to form an all-American fighter unit to be known as the Eagle Squadron. There was much cheering and toasting and it was far into the blacked-out night before the grand old group captain's party broke up.

Next morning dawned bright and cold. Piling into squad cars we started off for F. The eleven of us were a far different type of pilot than when we arrived at the training station several weeks before. We were ready, at last, for the front lines of the aerial battlefield.

We rolled along over low hills covered with stretches of thick woodlands and through fertile valleys in which were many pastures and occasionally a village. It was mid-October, and autumn had done some fine work with her paintbrush. The scenery was not unlike America's midwest. More stone had been used in buildings here than in our country, however. Here and there a surprising old castle frowned from some prominence.

Just outside a village we came on a roped-off section beside the road. Soldiers were on guard and inside the roped section were a half dozen men, peering at something on the ground. Around them dirt was piled high.

We stopped and learned a bomb disposal crew was at work, unearthing a time bomb. This sounded like unhealthy business, but our curiosity got the better of our caution so we went inside the ropes to have a look.

The crew of six evidently had finished their digging. They were looking in a hole, just wide enough for a small man to crawl into, which they had dug with pick and shovel into the semifrozen ground.

Standing at the edge of the shaft, we stared down. A little bald-headed man was dimly visible at the bottom of the hole, some fifteen feet below the ground level. He seemed to be resting against a black, finned object. Everyone was very quiet. I asked what the fellow was doing down there.

" 'E's listenin' to 'er tick," someone remarked as calmly as if " 'e" were a jeweler, fixing a clock. The speaker turned to us and, seeing the uniforms, he explained further.

"That pertic'l'r kinda bomb, sir, 'as a clock detonator. When she stops tickin', she's about ready to pop."

The bald head below tilted back and a grimy face called for a wrench. One was dropped to him. He caught it deftly and I heard the scraping of metal against metal as he applied the tool to a plug at the top end of the bomb.

The long dark plug was unscrewed and taken out, making the bomb harmless. In the plug was a cap, which was detonated by an electric charge. Somehow I felt a tension over my body ease. It's queer how taut your muscles get when you're standing over hundreds of pounds of dynamite that may explode any second. Once again I realized that ace aviators were not the only heroes of this war. Here, grubbing in the dark earth was heroism, as bright and shining as any I'd seen.

A rope was lowered and fastened around the ugly-looking bomb. The little expert with the wrench crawled out, being helped by his buddies. Four of us fellows gave the crew a hand in pulling out the missile. It was a 500-pounder.

"Pretty thing, ain't it?" somebody remarked. "Catchin' 'er before she went off will save a lot of windows in the village."

To keep their towns as warm and comfortable as possible these fellows risked their necks to make harmless a bomb that could have blown them all to bits in a split second. Hitler was wasting his terror methods on such people as these.

We climbed into the squad cars and continued on our way over winding roads and through several villages. About the only traffic we encountered were military motor lorries.

We arrived at F. and right away met the two men

who were to lead the new Eagle Squadron. One was Squadron Leader W. E. G. Taylor, an American from Kansas. The other was Squadron Leader, Walter Churchill, D.S.O., D.F.C., an Englishman. He had been decorated with the Distinguished Service Order and Distinguished Flying Cross for heroic service with the R.A.F. in France and during the evacuation at Dunkirk. They welcomed us and we were ordered to report immediately to the adjutant for our felt Eagles.

Without ceremony the adjutant handed them to us and we hurried to the fabric shop where they were sewn on both sleeves of our uniforms. The insignia consisted of a light blue eagle with outspread wings, one claw holding an olive branch and the other clutching arrows. The emblem had been approved by King George VI. Naturally, all of us were very proud to wear it.

I reported back to the squadron's leader's large office, in which were gathered more than a dozen pilots. Others were coming in as soon as they had their insignia sewn on.

Squadron Leader Churchill did some heavy introducing. I knew most of the boys for, of course, they had been in training with me. I greeted Phil Leckrone when he came in. He had been transferred from a

British squadron to the Eagles. There were four fellows I hadn't met before. One was Paul Anderson. He was the third Eagle from Sacramento, California, and had had considerable flying experience as a crop-dusting pilot.

The three others had gone from America to join the French Armée de l'Air. They had escaped to England just before France fell. One of them, Vernon "Shorty" Keough, was the smallest pilot I ever saw. He was less than five feet tall! Shorty's two pals were Andy Mamedoff, a husky, mustached man who fitted my idea of what a fighter pilot should look like, and Eugene Tobin, a big fellow with a determined cut to his chin. Shorty was from Brooklyn, Andy from Thompson, Connecticut, and Tobin from Los Angeles.

Here is the first roster of the Eagle Squadron as it formed that day in Squadron Leader Churchill's office: Luke Elbert Allen, Paul Roger Anderson, John Butler Ayer, Charles Edward Bateman, Gregory Augustus Daymond, Byron Fees Kennerly, Vernon Charles Keough, Stanley Michael Kolendorski, Philip Howard Leckrone, Andrew S. Mamedoff, James Leland McGinnis, Richard Arthur Moore, Edwin Ezell Orbison, Chesley Gordon Peterson, Dean Herbert Satterlee and Eugene Quimby

Tobin. The sixteen pilots ranged in age from nineteen to thirty-one. Gus Daymond was the youngest and I, the oldest.

Last but not least, the sixteen of us met the man who had as much to do with founding the squadron as anyone, Charles Sweeny, an American who bore the rank of honorary group captain in the Royal Air Force. Made honorary commander of the Eagle Squadron, he was the man who in 1925 assisted in reorganizing the Lafayette Escadrille of World War I to fight for France in Morocco. He told us how proud he was to have an all-American squadron in the R.A.F. to carry on the traditions of the old escadrille, the pilots of which he knew when he was serving in the French Foreign Legion. He said the new squadron represented the true pioneer spirit of the United States.

Thus was born America's aerial outpost of World War II.

That same day we were to have made our checkout flights in Hurricanes, but a heavy fog had rolled in, closing down the airdrome. We were keyed up for this important event. Postponement of the flight was quite a disappointment.

Since there was no flying to do, we strolled over to a famous near-by hotel. There we learned that America wasn't the only nation with an aerial outpost in Britain. It was in the warm, congenial atmosphere of the hotel's pub that we discovered some of the other "outposts." They were a group of tall, good-looking fellows wearing Royal Air Force uniforms with metal eagles hanging from chains over their left pockets. I wondered at first if this were another branch of the Eagle Squadron. When I asked one of the fellows about his insignia, he laughed and answered in a series of verbal explosions that sounded like Russian. At least it was near enough to Russian to be completely unintelligible to me.

Kolendorski came to my rescue. Being of Polish descent, he understood. The pilot was trying to tell me the eagle he wore was the Polish Eagle and that there were 1,800 of his countrymen in the R.A.F. What he didn't tell me was that they were among the best flyers in England. They'd had lots of combat experience, and because of what Germany had done to their families and homeland, they fought with the savageness of a wounded lion. One Polish squadron had more than 100 German planes to its credit.

The hotel's pub that afternoon was kind of an aerial international house. Besides British, American, and Polish pilots, there were a smattering of Czechs, Frenchmen, and a couple of Norwegians—all flyers.

Tobin had brought over a whole suitcase full of jazz records. We played them on the battered hotel phonograph. No matter what their nationality, everybody enjoyed the music. The favorite was "Roll Out the Barrel." Even the Czechs shouted the chorus of this. What they lacked in knowledge of English they made up by bellowing a rich "Yah! Yah! Yah—Yah—Yah!"

Enjoying the proceedings as much as any of us was the comely English barmaid, who, I guess, never before had had the pleasure of flirting with so many nationalities at once. She followed the custom of many English women, showing partiality to the Poles.

Especially hospitable to us Americans were these Poles, who continually offered us the addresses of pretty barmaids they had met during their leaves throughout England. They were doing their best to make us feel at home!

For two days fog prevented our making the checkout flight. To most of us it would be our first hop in a Hawker Hurricane, one of the world's fastest and most heavily armed interceptors. Of course in this flight we would be entirely on our own. No check pilot would be up with us to pull us out of a tight spot. And the Hurricane had several hundred horsepower more "oats" than the Master. It was planned that following these flights the squadron would be assigned to an operational airdrome. We had been given comfortable officers' quarters and instructed to be ready to fly as soon as weather permitted.

Meanwhile we got acquainted with the Hurricane. We paid several visits to the big, all-metal aircraft which were parked about the airdrome in dispersal bays. These bays are U-shaped concrete structures, without roofs, into which the aircraft are pushed. The concrete walls protect the machine from bomb explosions.

We took turns sitting in the cockpit and admiring the maze of instruments and levers. There was an instrument on the dash for everything but the pilot's blood pressure.

Probably the most interesting thing to us was the gunsight. This was a circle with a horizontal cross-hair. The sight had three controls, a key to flip on the electric juice which made the circle and cross-hair glow like miniature fluorescent tubes, the rheostat that controlled the intensity of the glow, and the dial which made the circle larger or smaller. If you were going to aim at a Messerschmitt 109, you set the dial for thirty-two feet, the wingspread of an Me. 109. When you looked through the circle at an Me. and its wings touched each side of the circle, you knew you were within range. Likewise, if you were going after a Heinkel 111 bomber, you set the dial for seventy-four feet, the wing span of that aircraft. When his wing tips touched each side of the circle you could start firing at him. Of course, to aim you moved the whole aircraft, since the guns were fixed in the wings, set so their fire would make a small circular cluster of hits about 250 yards away. From the Hurricane's eight machine guns tracer, incendiary, ball and armor-piercing bullets shot at the rate of 9,600 rounds a minute!

Of course, before you started shooting, you had to refer to the red firing button atop the small circular grip on the control stick. You had to turn the safety ring on it from the "safe" position to the "fire" position. To fire you pressed your right thumb on the button.

On the dashboard there were at least fifteen dials and gauges. On the left of the seat were three levers, mixture control, propeller pitch control, and the throttle. On the dash, in addition, there was an auxiliary throttle, or teat, which when pulled gives the aircraft a supersurge of power. To the pilot's right were two more levers, one for the flaps and the other for the undercarriage. Also, there were several keys which controlled the radio, magneto, oxygen, and so forth.

The control stick was "broken" just above the pilot's knees. To control his ailerons, he moved the top part of the stick from left to right. Inside the little wheel atop the stick was a lever, which when squeezed worked the air brakes.

The Hurricane is similar in performance to its smaller cousin, the Spitfire. There has been much rivalry between pilots of the two interceptors as to which is the better. I don't want to get into that argument. All I can say is that the crack Nazi squadrons found both Hurricane and Spitfire pilots and their machines plenty tough to deal with.

The afternoon of the third day the fog lifted somewhat. Our dampened spirits rose as a squadron leader came into the officers' mess and announced:

"Visibility still is bad, but we're going to check at least three of you out today." It was good to hear my name among those called.

I hurried into a pair of teddy bears—the thick silk linings to flying uniforms—and a fireproof sidka or coverall flying suit. On an extra cold day you can wear, instead, a fur-lined Irving suit.

I climbed into a parachute harness and pulled on the heavy helmet, to which were attached earphones, a microphone, and oxygen mask. The oxygen nose-piece was built into the microphone. Tubes and wires dangled from the helmet. In this heavy gear we ran outside as though we'd received a scramble call. "Scramble" is R.A.F. for battle.

I was surprised at the amount of fog as we stepped outside. There was a thick gray ceiling overhead and patches of gray reaching almost to the ground. It wouldn't pay to go far from the airdrome today. I didn't want to get lost in my first Hurricane flight. This first hop would be a pleasure to remember and something for the C.O., the commanding officer, to be proud of—I hoped!

A big gang of pilots, mostly in officers' caps and overcoats, were out there to wish us well. The three of us got our final instructions. We were to take off, circle the airdrome and come in and land. While in the air we would be in contact with the ground by radio. My radio call designation was to be "Circus Two Zero." Saluting, I hurried to my aircraft, which was on the line, ready to take off.

The big Merlin Rolls Royce motor had been warmed up and was ticking beautifully as I climbed into the cockpit. My hands trembled a bit—yes, I was nervous—as I adjusted the Sutton harness. This harness, consisting of straps over the shoulders and down across the chest to the back, was the safety belt. You could adjust it so it held you tight against the seat-back. I pulled on the silk gloves, then the flying mittens and plugged the cord from my headgear into the radio. While I attached the oxygen tube to the pipes in the ship, I knew I wouldn't fly high enough this trip to use it.

The corporal of the runway was flashing a green lamp at me, meaning I was to take off first. I touched the throttle and eased off the brakes. The aircraft jumped ahead with a splitting roar. I felt the tail rise, then, as I cut the throttle, it settled down. It was like a fire-breathing bronco.

I had been warned not to open the throttle wide or the aircraft would "jump" off the ground. Even at half throttle she thundered down the runway like a mad thing. It took strength and steady hands and feet to keep her on course. She grew light on her wheels, bouncing once and staying in the air a second before settling. On the next bounce I eased back the stick with my wrist and we were off into the white fog. I retracted the wheels, flipped the radio key to send and called into the mike:

"Hello, Circus Control. Circus Two Zero airborne."

I flipped the key to receive, heard a crackling of electricity and the answer:

"Hello, Circus Two Zero. Circus Control calling. Understand you are air-borne. Listening out."

The ground operator thus signified he had heard me and was through talking for the moment. We were using for the first time the regular R.T. or radio transmission procedure employed by all combat units.

I set a course on the compass to circle the airdrome until the other pilots took off. Then I would land. A glance outside showed nothing but fog, which meant I had to rely entirely on instruments.

Flying this aircraft was the nearest thing to riding a rocket I could imagine. The plane responded to the slightest touch on stick and throttle. This gave me a strange feeling of power and exhilaration, as if nothing were impossible.

I banked her gently and went into a gradual turn at 240 miles an hour. A sharp turn would black you out before you could say Jack Robinson's first name, and I didn't care to experience it on my first hop. Just after word came over the radio that the other two pilots were off the field, I had nearly completed the circle that would bring me onto the runway. The altimeter read 600 feet as I cut the throttle a bit, lowered the landing gear and eased down the flaps. The aircraft began settling and gliding down. As yet nothing but fog was visible below. Over the radio had come the voices of the other two pilots, announc-

ing they were aloft so I knew it was safe to come in—
that is, if I could find the runway.

The aircraft was losing altitude alarmingly as I
flipped the radio key to send and called:

"Hello, Circus Control! Hello, Circus Control!
Circus Two Zero calling. Coming down for landing,
but can't see field. Am I near it?"

Flipping the key, I heard operations answer:

"Hello, Circus Two Zero. Circus Control calling.
Pancake! Pancake! You are over base."

Pancake meant to land. That was fine, but you can't
dock a ship if you can't see the wharf. My left hand
was on the throttle, ready to gun her if I saw she was
falling too fast.

Glancing back over the trailing edge of the starboard wing I saw a hedge dimly visible through the
fog. That was the field's boundary mark. It slid away.
Then two dispersal bays made their appearance for
a moment. I must be only sixty feet above the runway. From the way landmarks melted away into the
bright whiteness, I knew the fog was closing in. We
had to get down before it wiped out the landmarks
completely.

The Hurricane wasn't settling fast enough so I
nosed her down a little. Even with flaps and undercarriage down she picked up speed and I knew I
would overshoot the field. So I gunned her.

Instantly she responded to the throttle and roared ahead in a gradual climbing turn. I set a compass course that would bring me over the base again. Through the R.T. I heard operations tell one of the other fellows to pancake. I wasn't the only one bothered by the "invisibility." The radios on our three fog-bound aircraft as well as the operator's set were tuned to the same wave length so we could hear each other.

Waiting until the radio conversation was finished, I called:

"Hello, Circus Control. Circus Two Zero calling. Are you receiving me?"

"Hello, Circus Two Zero. Circus Control answering. Receiving you loud and clear. Go ahead Circus Two Zero."

"Hello, Circus Control. Circus Two Zero. Am making 180-degree circle to come in again for landing."

"Hello, Circus Two Zero. Circus Control answering. O.K. and listening out."

I heard one of the boys muttering into his mike something about the fog making a three-ring circus of our maiden hops in Hurricanes. The principal thing that worried me was meeting one of them in this fog. A collision in this soup would be a very possible but unhappy event.

The instruments told me I was nearing the field again, so I started down. I looked over the trailing edge of the wing just in time to see a tree top slide past perhaps fifty feet below. That was a good sign. At least I was approaching the ground. Then below some brush came into view. There wasn't any brush on the field! I must be lost. Because of the increased drag on the aircraft caused by the undercarriage and flaps being down, the motor temperature gauge began acting up. The motor was heating badly. Shortly the glycol, freeze-proof cooling liquid in the radiator, would start to boil. Then the motor would freeze, causing the motor to stall. Then—pleasant thoughts, these. Thank heaven I didn't have time to give them serious attention.

Again I gunned her and lifted her nose. Where the devil was I? The whiteness all around was getting on my nerves a little. Then I realized what had happened. In keeping an eye out for the ground, I unconsciously had made the plane turn the way I was looking, it was so sensitive to the controls. Now that I was off the flight pattern of the field the chances of running into the other boys were greater than ever.

I must keep my eyes on the instruments. They're the only reliable senses of a pilot when he's flying blind. If I'd kept on looking outside, I might end

[106]

up flying upside down and never know it. While I had no idea where I was, operations could follow my flight through a radio device on my aircraft.

"Hello, Circus Control," I called. "Circus Two Zero calling. Give me a vector."

A vector is a compass reading to direct me to the base.

"Hello, Circus Two Zero. Circus Control answering. Vector eight six."

Almost as soon as I set the compass, operations called with, "Pancake! Pancake! Circus Two Zero. You are over base!"

I came down just in time to see the tall hedge on the far end of the field slide away. I had to go up again. The temperature gauge showed the glycol was boiling. The oil pressure was dropping off alarmingly.

I was very careful about the circle this time. When operations ordered "pancake!" I came down sharply, although I couldn't see a thing but the monotonous gray-white mist. Correcting for any turn I might put the aircraft into by looking out, I shot a glance over my wing. There was the hedge. I wasn't going to let the ground slide away from under me this time.

Down we came at a little more than 100 miles an hour. There was the turf not ten feet below. I must make it this time. With throttle back, the aircraft settled onto the ground and I felt the welcome grating of wheels on turf. Whew! The plane was traveling a little too fast and I squeezed the brake control gently. They couldn't be applied too strongly or the aircraft would nose over.

The aircraft covered the rest of the runway in no time at all. Because I couldn't stop her too suddenly, I had to sit there and ride with her over the end of the runway into some marshy muck. I felt her sink to starboard, the propeller kicking up a sheet of mud that plastered the windscreen.

Kicking starboard rudder and giving her the gun, I squeezed the brake handle tight. Giving her starboard rudder locked the starboard wheel but didn't apply any brake to the port wheel. The aircraft lumbered around in a sharp turn, the propeller throwing up a lot of mud. The motor responded sluggishly because it was badly overheated.

I taxied up the side of the field and stopped in front of the Hurricane's dispersal bay.

Several dim figures were running through the murk. It was some of the boys, who were going to have some fun at my mud-covered expense. I slid open the hatch, unfastened the Sutton harness and crawled out. Somehow I felt limp as a rag.

"Nice landing, Kenn'ly," a squadron leader commented as I felt the pleasantly solid earth under my feet. "A real job coming down in this soup."

The other two pilots had landed during the time I was lost. The three of us decided we required a little more experience in a fog before we could call such a landing fun.

The next few days, while we still were waiting to be transferred to our fighter airdrome, we got some more experience fog-flying. One of those flights was almost my last!

At the airdrome were some Brewster Buffalo single-seated fighters that had been made in the United States for France. They were brought to England from France when the Nazi hordes were taking that country. Appropriately called "the flying barrels" because of their thick, stubby fuselage, the long-range fighters were very fast and extremely maneuverable.

Shorty Keough, who, of course, had been in France with Tobin and Mamedoff, showed me one. The instruments were in French, with metric markings. Shorty tried to explain to me what the French markings meant, but I noticed he had marked in red ink the spots on the dials where he wanted the needles to be in flight. This led me to believe he wasn't too sure of the "parley vous" readings.

[109]

Anyhow, I wanted to fly one of the Buffaloes. The C.O. gave his consent. That was one grand thing I noticed at English airdromes. If you wanted to fly an aircraft, all you had to do was ask. There was no red tape about it.

One afternoon I took off, secretly hoping I'd run into a Jerry. There was a high fog but plenty of ceiling for a landing. Smaller than even a Spitfire and livelier than an unbroken colt, the aircraft took me for a steep ride above the fog. A section of Hurricanes and later one of Spitfires passed me on their way to patrol the English Channel. However I was unable to spot any Nazis, so somewhere near the east coast I came down for a look at the scenery. There were patches of mist near the ground and I took her through a couple of them at about 270 miles an hour. I flew near one city and skirted it low to avoid the barrage balloon cables. There were several canals in the area. I struck a long stretch of low fog and rocketed through it in a gradual curve. Because of the "français" on the altimeter, I didn't know the altitude, but knew it must be kind of low.

Suddenly the mist parted. Strangely, I was flying only a few feet above water. Looking out the hatch to right and left, I saw brown-colored walls slanting into the water. The Buffalo was following a great curve of the walls, the tops of which were just above the level of my tail. As I pulled the Buffalo up, the walls gave way to meadows and pastures. I could feel the hairs rising inside my helmet as I realized I had been flying in a canal! Somehow in that mist I had dropped below the level of the ground. Miraculously, the ground hadn't been there. Still more miraculously, the aircraft was following the curve of the canal!

Before I went back to the base, I circled around in the sky for awhile, cooling off and thanking my guardian angel, or whoever it was that guided the Buffalo through that canal in the fog.

Chapter VII

EAGLES' NEST

FINALLY, late in October came the orders to report to a fighter airdrome in northern England. At last the Eagles were to have a nest! There was much congratulating all around, and several British pilots we had met wished us "lots of victories."

The first thing we saw as we approached the big fighter 'drome was an American flag flying proudly against the blue sky. Beside it on another mast flew the Union Jack. These flags flying together symbolized to me what most of us pilots felt at the time: It wouldn't be long before the two great democracies would be fighting side by side against our common foe.

I was surprised at the large size of the airdrome. There were several hangars and other buildings surrounding the grass landing field. It was an older 'drome than the others where we'd been stationed, and the officers' quarters where we were housed were of brick. While the airdrome was plainly visible when you approached it from the ground, I was astonished, the first time I went up, to see how skillfully it had been camouflaged so as to blend into the beautiful countryside. Unless you knew where it was, it would be impossible to find it from the air, even if you were only a few thousand feet up.

Nearly 2,500 people were stationed there, including pilots for three fighter squadrons, ground personnel for the aircraft, and soldiers. Always, there were at least twenty-five planes dispersed over the field, parked in dispersal bays. Like other British fighters, these were all camouflaged with wavy designs of brown and green on top and gray underneath. The 'drome was equipped to base a squadron of Spitfires, one of Hurricanes, and one of Defiants. The Defiants are tough two-seated night fighters and were painted the color of a blackout. We inspected them shortly after we arrived. Behind the pilot's cockpit was a glazed, domed, power-operated gun turret. The second man sat inside it.

An aircraftsman who was inspecting the engine of one of them proudly informed us that the first time the Defiants made their appearance over Dunkirk, during the evacuation, a full squadron of them downed nearly forty Messerschmitts. Unfamiliar with the turret, which could fire over the tail of the Defiants, the Nazis came at them from the rear and were blasted out of the sky before they knew what hit them. Hurricanes and Spitfires being a little faster, the Defiants had been assigned to night fighting chiefly.

We were taken to a one-story wooden building just at the edge of the field. We entered by a doorway that faced the field and met more than a dozen British fighter pilots, dressed in full flying gear. They were "in readiness" for a scramble call. The large room was fitted out with several big chairs and cots, a large wood stove, and a radio. Along one wall were parachute racks. Scattered about the room were miniature models of German aircraft with their vulnerable parts plainly marked. We recognized models of Messerschmitt 109's and 110's, Junkers 88's, Dornier 17's, and Heinkel 111's, the principal types of aircraft the Nazis were using over Britain at the time. There were models of other planes that we were less familiar with.

This was the room, called the dispersal hut, where we would wait, while on duty, for a scramble. The hut was known as one of the two "offices" of a fighter pilot. His other office was his cockpit, which often was called the "greenhouse" because it was glass-enclosed.

We left the hut to be assigned our aircraft. I got a brand new Hurricane, which no one else was supposed to fly. Shortly afterwards I had my name and the Eagle Squadron insignia put on it. Along with the aircraft, we each had assigned to us a ground crew of eight aircraftsmen. Their job was to keep the aircraft in top shape. The crew included an electrician, mechanic, armorer and fitter, all under the command of a flight sergeant.

We discovered that these ground crews worshiped their planes and pilots and would fight at the drop of a hat if anybody said anything against either. It was great to have such a loyal rooting section. Every night when the pilot is relieved from readiness—goes off duty—his crew swarms over the aircraft, re-fueling, greasing, reloading the eight machine-guns, checking instruments and control wires, in fact, giving her a very thorough going over. Just before the pilot goes on duty, he checks the aircraft himself, just for good measure. After all, it's his neck if any one of a hundred things goes wrong.

Our routine called for our being awakened about an hour before dawn by our batman. Each of us, since we were officers, had one of these valets. As soon as we had dressed and eaten breakfast we were to inspect our aircraft. If everything was O.K., we were to sign in and remain in the dispersal hut on duty until sunset, except for meals and afternoon tea. At that time the night fighters would take over.

This was a long stretch in summer, when you have to get up about 5 A.M. and are on duty until 10:30 P.M. It wasn't so bad, however, this late in the year.

There being sixteen in our squadron, a dozen of us were active pilots with four in reserve. A full squadron is twelve men, with usually another six in reserve. We were to take turns being on the reserve list.

Luke and I were given the same room. Being from a warm part of the United States and not yet fully acclimated to a British winter, the two of us had lots of fun trying to coax heat from the steam radiator. There's nothing cooler than an English radiator, just as there's nothing warmer than an English hearth.

The day following our arrival we were awakened by our batman. It was still dark out and we had a struggle to wake up. He brought us each a cup of tea. From that morning on I have recommended tea as a "waker-upper." We climbed into complete flying gear and had to waddle down to breakfast to navigate in all the clothes.

After a breakfast of porridge, smoked herring, white bread and coffee, the C.O. turned to Jim Mc-Ginnis and me and asked, "How would you chaps like to do a bit of cloud flying?"

We thought we were through with training flights and weren't sure what the C.O. meant by "cloud flight," but it sounded like another flying lesson.

Jim and I said we'd try it and the C.O. nodded and added, "Fine, we'll have three Spitfires warmed up to take off at daylight."

Spitfires! That sounded like a good show so Jim and I hurried out with the C.O. to look over the aircraft before we took off. Daylight was breaking as we reached the Spits in their dispersal bays. It was my first early morning inspection and since, in addition, this was an unfamiliar aircraft, the ground crew of the plane went over her with me. Everything was shipshape, including the eight machine guns. They were fully loaded.

The C.O. said woe betide any Jerries we might encounter, for a section of Hurricane pilots in Spitfires was too much for any enemy to ask for.

The sun peeped over the horizon, slanting gargantuan shadows across the wide turf field. As I climbed into the Spitfire, I noticed heavy clouds overhead. Somehow I didn't feel as if I were getting into a strange plane at all. It corresponded closely to the Hurricane, except for a slight difference in the gun-sight, which the C.O. explained to me. Both aircraft have the same firing power.

The crews pushed the Spitfires out of the bays and swung them around. The big Merlin motors already had been warmed up. I turned on the ignition and, with a couple of powerful coughs, she came to life, ticking over the three-bladed propeller. I plugged in the radio and oxygen, being careful not to tangle the cords. I knew we were in for some high-flying and I'd need the oxygen.

The C.O. gave the signal and, as I gunned her, two aircraftsmen followed and pushed the elliptical wings so the plane would point into the wind for the take-off. The lead Spitfire roared ahead and Jim and I pulled in behind, saluting the aircraftsmen as they saluted us. Down the field we thundered. I was number two man on the C.O.'s right and Jim number three on his left. We took off.

I had to keep my eyes sharp on the C.O.'s star-board wing. He was pulling up very fast and turning steeply to starboard. I dropped below him to keep in position. Jim had to climb above on the other side, keeping level with the leader's port wing. We were flying as one plane, Jim and I were rising and falling with our targets, which were the front Spitfire's

[118]

wings. I was glad for what close formation experience
I had had because when we hit the clouds we'd have
to stick within reaching distance of the C.O. to keep
from losing him. I was over-controlling a little on
the ailerons. The Spitfire was lighter on them than
the Hurricane, this being the only difference I noticed
in the flying characteristics of the two.

We made for the clouds as quickly as possible. Soon
we were enveloped by them. I could just see the nose
of the C.O.'s aircraft as my port wing was six feet
back of his starboard wing.

Suddenly his wing seemed to lift right up into the
soup, growing misty as it drew away. I needled her,
or pulled the auxiliary throttle, and followed on up.
At the same time I leaned heavily against the Sutton
harness and pulled up my diaphragm to offset any
tendency to black out.

I caught up with him as he leveled off and glanced
at Jim's ship. He was leaning forward determinedly
in his glazed cockpit. I was about ready to cut the
throttle a little but I noticed I was just keeping up
with the leader. The altimeter read 6,500, and the
speedometer 312 miles an hour. I guessed the C.O.
was trying to run away from us. Three could play at
that game. I switched on the oxygen, wanting plenty
of that juice if he were going to play rough.

Abruptly the C.O. pulled up again. We were rock-

[119]

eting so fast that I slid far under him before I could come up. The controls worked stiffly because of the speed. Then I shot up almost vertically. Where was everybody!

In a second I was alone in the fog. Somewhere near, perhaps only a few feet away, were two other Spitfires, screaming through the shroud of moisture. A collision would mean a split-second tragedy. My aircraft still was almost in vertical flight. A shadowy something was over me and I looked up quickly.

It was the wing tip of a Spitfire, a bare yard over mine! Quickly I shoved the stick ahead and felt myself rising in the seat as centrifugal force tried to lift me out of the plane.

There was a crackling in my ears as someone snapped on the radio.

"Hey there, Kenn'ly!" It was the C.O.'s voice. He was flying level now and I had unconsciously cut the throttle and was pulling back in position behind him.

"You shook me to the core that time!" he barked.

For the next thirty minutes we played tag in the clouds. I began to sweat. My eyes could have been knocked off with a stick, they were popping out so far, trying to keep the C.O.'s starboard wing in view. My right hand was glued to the stick, I knew we'd need a crowbar to pry it loose. We turned, climbed,

[120]

dove. The entire time we couldn't see more than fifty feet ahead except for a few brief respites when we shot out of one cloud into the next one. We were sure being put through the ropes.

I didn't even dare to look at the dashboard to see how much petrol was left. A quick glance from that wing might mean I'd lose it completely. All this time McGinnis was clinging by the C.O.'s other wing.

Finally our leader called for a line astern formation, ordering me into the number three position at the tail with Jim as number two man in between. Now my objective was the tail of Jim's plane. I couldn't even see the C.O. He was ahead of Jim, shrouded in fog.

Jim dropped away in a dive and I followed. As we darted under the clouds, I felt like a blind man whose sight suddenly is restored. There, a scant 5,000 feet below, lay the gray landscape of England. Now I spotted the C.O. The outline of his wings grew from a razor line to an ellipse, revealing that he was coming out of his dive.

I'd had enough of clouds, but evidently the C.O. hadn't, for he swept gracefully into a light, shreddy mist that hung below the base of a big cumulus. I kept my eye on Jim as we hit it. Jim pulled to the left and I kept on his tail. Then he zoomed up to where the mist was thick and disappeared. Keeping hot on his trail, I needled her to catch up; I'd lost him for a second.

I whipped out of the moisture and there, coming straight at me and growing larger horribly fast was a Spitfire! I banked hard to starboard in a sickening maneuver that threw the aircraft up on end. I saw the black streaks of my eyelashes, the first symptom of blacking out. The other ship rolled over the other way and turned hard around. We were past each other in an instant since our combined speeds were something like 500 miles an hour. Another narrow squeak!

Quickly pulling back the throttle, I put her into a mild climb to slow down. I'd begun to sag forward but snapped out immediately after stopping the turn.

The C.O.'s voice crackled over the earphones:

"What the devil, Kenn'ly! If you had been trailing me in that light stuff, instead of number two man, you would have stayed with me. As it was, one man gets lost and the whole formation breaks up. Keep your eye on the leader whenever you can!"

Snapping the key to send I answered a meek, "Yes, sir." I felt that this was superfluous. Later I found out this was the most valuable point in formation flying I ever learned.

Glancing around I saw the C.O. coming up on my

right side about fifty feet above. I pulled in behind him and looked around for Jim. There was a fighter-type plane about four miles away and headed for us. It looked like a Spitfire so we headed for it.

Over the radio came Jim's voice:

"You got away from us, sir."

"Yes, but I don't think Jerry would have such an easy job of it," the C.O. answered. He always knew how to say some little thing that brought you out of a mental tailspin.

"Let's take a look over the North Sea. We may run into a Jerry," he said as Jim moved his Spitfire into line astern in front of me. We headed east below the clouds.

The C.O. called operations and asked if there was "any business" along the coast. Operations answered that three bandits—enemy aircraft—had attempted to machine-gun the town of Leeds and were being chased by a patrol squadron of Spitfires. This town was inland and if we stepped on it we might arrive in time to get in on the show.

The C.O. asked for a vector and led us up through the clouds to the northeast. Atop the clouds we came into the brilliant sunlight and continued on up to 20,000 feet, then leveled off. The C.O. was needling her, for we had to make time. The speedometer climbed above 360 miles an hour, the fastest I'd ever flown. We were traveling in a loose formation now that we were above the clouds so I didn't have to concentrate too much on the aircraft ahead to stay with them. This gave me time to look around for the Jerries. My chief job, though, as rear man, was to weave a little and keep a sharp lookout through the rear view mirror for a possible attack on our stern. My position was called "rear man Charley."

Jim's voice came over the radio: "Bandits off the port wing!"

I looked and saw three black specks in a vic about five miles away and some 5,000 feet below us. There were no clouds in their immediate vicinity and they were rocketing for the safety of the clouds below us. Perhaps a mile behind them were three more specks in single file; they must be Spitfires.

Never having seen a German plane from the air, I could hardly believe that these were the hated Nazis below us.

The C.O. headed for them and went into a shallow dive. As we followed down, I turned on the gunsight and moved the firing button guard from the "safe" to "firing" position.

Evidently seeing us slanting at them, the Jerries banked away and headed due east, forgetting about

the clouds. The C.O. banked ever so slightly, no doubt
to keep Jim and me from blacking out, and roared
northeast. I was as tense as a wound-up clock spring.
My lips got dry.

By turning, the Jerries allowed the chasing Spitfires to come in on them. But the Nazis didn't stop to
fight. Their vic broke apart and they began twisting
and diving. I knew they were Messerschmitt 109's
from their size and square-cut wing tips. Black crosses
were plainly visible on their blue-gray wings as they
turned and twisted.

One Jerry shot out a blob of black smoke and went
into a dive. With the next clot of smoke was a jet of
fire. A Spitfire caught up with another Me., literally
blasting its tail to pieces. Parts of it scattered in the
sky, like feathers shot from a blackbird. The remaining Jerry headed east, wide open. One Spitfire
was after him, about a mile behind. The other two
were climbing up after their ferocious attacks. I
hoped we'd join in the chase to try and make the
bag 100 per cent.

"Kenn'ly and McGinnis!" came the C.O.'s voice
over the R.T., "close formation. The bandit's too far
out."

That meant we weren't going after him. Before
either Jim or I could think up a diplomatic protest

[125]

to this order, the C.O. banked gradually in a shallow glide. We cut our throttles and followed. I got a last glimpse of the Jerry, still high-tailing it for home over the North Sea, the Spitfire in pursuit.

Glancing at my petrol gauge I was surprised to find the tanks almost empty. The smart C.O. must have thought of this when he ordered us back. He didn't want us stranded out somewhere over the North Sea! I turned off the gunsight and twisted the firing button guard to the "safe" position.

After we had landed at our airdrome, I felt tired from the strain of flying so fast.

That night in the officer's lounge we heard Lord Haw Haw, the Nazi commentator with the deep British voice, describe on the radio how three Messerschmitt 109's, two of them carrying bombs, had caused damage to factories at Leeds and, on the return trip, had downed three out of twelve Spitfires that attacked them. He reported that all three Messerschmitts returned safely to their base. The only correct information given was the number of Me.'s and the time of the flight. We were there, Lord Haw Haw, and saw a different story! But unlike us, who could listen without restrictions to enemy broadcasts, the families of the two Nazis who were shot down were not allowed to listen to our broadcasts of what actually happened.

1. Byron Kennerly as a pilot officer in the Eagle Squadron, R.A.F.

2. The author in a Ryan training plane at Mines Field, California, before the war.

3a. Three sections of Miles Master training planes being flown by Americans shortly before the Eagle Squadron was formed.

3b. Aerial marksmanship is groomed by ground practice. A British sergeant pilot demonstrates a fast-firing gun to Eagle Squadron pilots.

4. Pilot Officer William Nichols of San Carlos, California, beside his Hurricane. The aircraft wears a Mickey Mouse version of the Eagle insignia. This pilot was reported to have been shot down and taken prisoner.

5. The "kid" and "grandpappy" of the Eagle Squadron standing in front of a Miles Master training plane. In other words, "Gus" Daymond and myself.

6. In front of the officers' mess are nine members of the Eagle Squadron. Seated in front are five of the Squadron's British officers. Standing, left to right, are Stanley Michael Kolendorski (killed), Gregory Augustus Daymond, Vernon Charles Keough (killed), Andrew Mamedoff

7. Charles Sweeny, made honorary squadron leader of the Eagle Squadron because of his major part in founding the all-American interceptor unit.

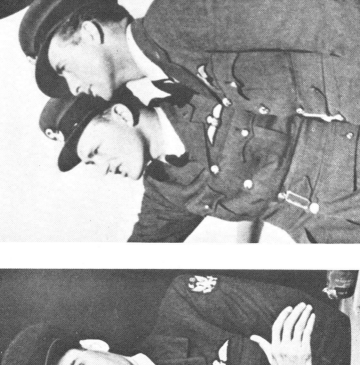

8a. Squadron Leader William Erwin Gibson Taylor

8b. "Bud" Orbison and I watch one of the boys

© *Acme Newspictures, Inc.*

9. An Eagle pilot ready to take off for a patrol after his Hurricane has been refueled.

10a. Pilot Officer James McGinnis stands beside his Hurricane in the snow.

10b. On another chilly day, "Pete" Peterson wears the jacket to a fur-lined Irving suit, while I'm dressed in a sidka, or coverall flying suit.

© *Acme Newspictures, Inc.*

11. Pilots of the Eagle Squadron on the march with Squadron Leader W. E. G. Taylor, fourth from left. One of the squadron's powerful Hawker Hurricane interceptors is in the background.

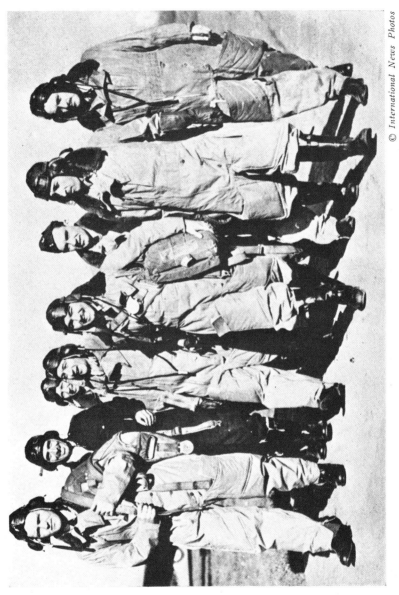

Off for a patrol are Eagle pilots, left to right, "Bud" Orbison, "Jack" Kennerly, "Pete"

13. Running out to their fighter planes to answer a "scramble" call are, left to right, Eugene Tobin, Peter Provenzano, Samuel Mauriello and Luke Allen.

14. Two Eagle aces, "Gus" Daymond, left, and "Pete" Peterson. Both have been awarded the

15. Attired in their "Mae West" life jackets, members of the Second American Eagle Squadron take time off from flying to pose for a picture with their mascot, "Rinzo," at the "Eagles' Nest" in England.

16. The Eagles Roar!

Nazi propaganda of an even more flagrant kind caused one Jerry pilot no end of embarrassment. He landed his fighter at an airdrome near ours in broad daylight. As he came in with wheels and flaps down— usually a sign of surrender—the antiaircraft gunners held their fire.

But this Jerry wasn't surrendering. Carrying a suitcase, he jauntily climbed from his Me. and demanded in broken English to be directed to the nearest Nazi airdrome. He had been led to believe that most of England was in German hands!

Unfortunately, for awhile after we arrived at our fighter station, there wasn't much air action for us. Because of their tremendous losses, the Jerries had discontinued mass daylight raids and had stepped up their night bombing. Their chief daylight activity was over Kent, where fleets of high-flying fighters, some of them carrying small bombs, tried to do some damage. Apparently they were convinced they couldn't blast the R.A.F. out of the sky.

While there wasn't much flying for us to do, the British did their best to make our time pass pleasantly. They even attempted to bring California sunshine to the eight of us who were from that state by sending the squadron a sun lamp! It's surprising how the lamp helped us retain our fast fading sun tan.

A London woman presented us with a combination radio and phonograph. Gene Tobin's jazz records were just about worn out on it.

Then, like Mickey Mouse and other movie stars, we began getting fan mail and requests for autographs. I don't know why because we really hadn't gotten into action yet. One bedridden elderly English woman had written to the C.O., asking my name. She said she had seen my picture with some of the other boys in a newspaper. She asked for an autographed photograph of me and I sent her one. Whereupon, she sent me two balaclavas, beautifully knitted in Royal Air Force blue. These are hoods, covering the head, shoulders and chest, with a slit in the head for the eyes. It seems that when knighthood was in flower, ladies gave these to their knights to wear into battle. It was wonderful of this kindly friend, whom I never was fortunate enough to meet, to send them.

However, I couldn't wear knitted hoods in a plane and, to make the best possible use of them, I gave them to two members of my crew. They wore the hoods when they lay on the tail of my Hurricane while I warmed up the motor. They had to do this, otherwise the propeller blast would lift the tail high in the air. Many mornings there was as much as six inches of snow on the ground and the hoods protected the men's faces as the sleet blasted back at them.

Then I got a letter from an eighteen-year-old girl in the United States. She wrote that she wanted "to know all about England." For a moment, the letter made me feel much younger than my thirty-one years. All the fellows got similar letters and presents.

Besides entertaining us in their homes, the British gave many parties for us. There was a dance every Friday night in the noncommissioned officers' quarters. Every Saturday night a vaudeville show or band concert was held. We had our own station band, made up of English musicians who were in the R.A.F.

It was at one of these concerts that some English girls, members of what we called the "land army"— a group of girls who wore overalls and did farm work for defense—suggested a hamburger party. They'd heard us talk about "hamburgers" and wanted to try some. Four of us fellows bought steaks, took them to one of the girls' houses, ground them up and cooked them. The ensuing dish was a big success, even if we did have to use bread instead of buns! It was at this hamburger affair that I discovered about every other English girl was named either Sheila or Peggy.

When the British learned that Shorty Keough was a parachute expert, he was put to work lecturing on packing, wearing, and landing in 'chutes. Shorty knew his business, for he was a veteran of 486 jumps in America. He maintained that once he had been a normal sized man, but the continual landing in a parachute had had the effect of compressing him down, like the action of a pile driver, to a scant five feet.

"The main reason I like this parachute business," he would say, "is because you never get complaints from dissatisfied customers."

Often sections of the squadron were relieved from readiness to attend one of these parachute lectures, or to hear lectures by R.A.F. officers on gunnery, use of oxygen in high altitudes or other phases of aerial combat. Somehow we didn't have to take notes on what was said. Perhaps this was because remembering might mean saving your life or the life of a pal.

We also attended motion picture showings. The British call them cinemas. Although the pictures were extremely interesting, they weren't put on for entertainment. They taught us how to bring down big game and, in turn, escape being brought down. Each Spitfire and Hurricane carries a motion picture camera. Its view finder is the gunsight. When you press the firing button in combat, the camera automatically starts grinding. The pictures show the enemy aircraft, provided he is in the gunsight, and the path of your tracer bullets. Developed and thrown on a screen, the photographs reveal why you did or did not bring down the target. The pictures are accompanied by a talk from an officer. We saw several cinemas of combats in which British pilots at our station had been engaged.

Sometimes we were ordered aloft to practice advanced combat maneuvers. For this we used the camera. Later we studied the pictures and were shown where we were right or wrong in executing our practice tactics.

For fellows who "pulled butches" during practice, the squadron had its own way of dressing them down. The American who was the "pin-point" expert still got lost occasionally and would call operations anxiously for a vector home.

When he would arrive in the dispersal hut, we would stop our conversation or cards or whatever we were doing, and just sit there silently, some of us staring disappointedly at him. The fellow would go from one to another trying to strike up a conversation. But we were silent. Finally he would blow his top off, admitting he'd gotten lost, and we'd have a laugh. We'd almost rather have an officer tear a strip off us than to run the squadron's "gantlet of silence."

One pilot had a little "trouble" of a different kind during his first weeks at the station. It was Gus Daymond, the nineteen-year-old youngster of the squadron. He looked his age and this worried him. Doggedly he kept shaving with a safety razor, hoping each day he might harvest at least a trace of a crop. One day I removed the blade from his razor. For a week he continued his bladeless shaving, finally discovering what had happened. Whenever he appeared, the fellows would start feeling their chins and sadly shake their heads. For several days he refused to speak to me. Although at that time Gus didn't have any whiskers, he was all man and quickly developed into one of the ace pilots of the Eagle Squadron.

One morning we were scheduled to go up for heavy combat attack practice with three sections of Handley Page Hampden bombers. However, this wasn't the topic of conversation at the breakfast table. The boys were discussing a visitor who had landed at the airdrome the night before.

There had been a drizzling fog most of the night and several Handley Page Hampdens, returning from a sweep over Nazi-occupied territory, had become lost in the murk. Our airdrome had been notified that some of them might come in to land on our field.

Soon after this notification, the corporal of the flare path heard a bomber overhead. Figuring it was too foggy to see an answer to his challenge rocket, he lighted the flare path. A huge aircraft came down out of the darkness, taxied along the runway and stopped in front of the corporal, who was waving a flashlight to direct the bomber to the end of the runway.

A door in the bomber opened, a pilot climbed out and asked a question. The corporal asked him to repeat it, the idling motors evidently preventing his hearing the question. The pilot asked in broken English, "What airdrome is this?"

The corporal glanced at the glass nose of the bomber and was shocked to see a double machine gun trained on him. Then he saw a big cross on the under side of the wing.

Without waiting for an answer, the pilot hopped back into the cabin, the big aircraft roared around, its port motor bursting with noisy power. Then the plane took off into the glistening wet night.

The corporal snapped off the flare path and sounded the air raid alarm. But no bombs were dropped. Something did drop, however, for a section

[133]

of Defiants took off immediately, caught the bomber over the North Sea where there was no fog and brought it down. That Jerry landed on the wrong airdrome!

By midmorning the mist of the night before had dissipated, leaving the sky as clear as crystal. Twelve of us took off in four vics for a rendezvous with the Hampdens at 15,000 feet. Our Browning machine-guns were not loaded, but we carried plenty of film in the cine-cameras to record our marksmanship. The bombers, likewise, would be "shooting" at us with cameras. We were to practice the four principal interceptor attacks on bombers: The beam, belly, head-on and quarter attacks. I adjusted my Sutton harness, leaving it fairly loose so I could lean forward in the turning dives and to resist blacking out, knowing that today I would experience not one but several blackouts.

When we reached about 12,000 feet we spotted the Hampdens above us, clipping along at about 180 miles an hour in three sections. While they were bunched enough so that a fighter diving in the center of them would receive the cross-fire from all nine bombers, they were far enough apart so that any one bomber could take evasive action to throw off a fighter's aim. Sage pilots, these Hampden boys. I

[134]

knew we'd have to do some tall flying to register hits on them without getting it in the neck ourselves.

We spiraled up to 18,000 feet, 3,000 feet above them. The C.O., who was leading our squadron, made certain we were flying between the Hampdens and the sun. At 18,000 we leveled off. I could see the C.O. was getting us in position for a beam attack, the most vicious and dangerous attack of all to a bomber. The maneuver consisted of a dive, leveling off into a slow roll toward the side of the bomber. When you were in range of the bomber, or about 250 yards away, you were rolling and almost upside down. Then you'd open fire and give him the "works." The idea was to be upside down when you crossed under the bomber's nose. Then you dove out of it, dropping away about 6,000 feet and blacking out momentarily. You couldn't prevent the speed of the break-away from knocking you cold. The attack was effective because it allowed the gunner on the bombers so little time to get a bead on you. By the time the rear gunner had aimed at you, you were past him, and when the front gunner could take aim, you were down and out of range. The fighter pilot's object was to wing the bomber pilot.

The C.O. peeled off in a beautiful power dive. The rest of us followed, fanning out as we selected our targets. I came out of the dive just below 15,000 feet and headed for my target, rolling over as I did so. When the sights showed I was in range, I pressed the firing button. The physical strain was terrific in keeping the sights just ahead of the pilot—allowing for deflection of aim—while the Hurricane was rolling over on its back. I'd tried to come in with the sun so the gunners would have a hard time spotting me. If you don't think it's difficult to spot an airplane against the sun, try it sometime.

A few yards from the bomber, I pulled down and slid across under it, the bellies of the two aircraft only a few feet apart. Then I pulled her into a dive and for a moment saw the streaks of my eyelashes. My eyelids seemed to weigh a ton apiece as they closed. I was tensing my abdomen and leaning forward in the Sutton harness. But it was no use. I felt myself sag into the seat. Then oblivion.

Finally coming to I found the aircraft in a roaring dive. Streamers of pain shot through my head from the sudden drop in altitude. Weakly, at first, I pulled her out. The controls worked stiffly at 480 miles an hour. The altimeter read 8,000 feet.

This had been my first actual blackout. I had dreaded experiencing it, fearful lest I wouldn't regain consciousness before hitting the deck. But it was something every fighter pilot must become accustomed to. Modern interceptors are so fast that it's impossible to make a sharp turn in one without centrifugal force draining the blood from your head and causing you to faint momentarily.

My strength came back quickly as the Hurricane vaulted upstairs. The pain in my head left when I leveled off at 18,000 feet. There were the bombers coming around in a gradual circle. Some half dozen Hurricanes already were at my level and others were on the way up.

As soon as the rest of the interceptors reached us we reformed and went down again. This time when I closed in on a bomber and began the roll, the bomber dropped slightly to evade my aim. I started to bring the nose down a little to get a bead on him but the gray curtain closed down. A change in course of only a few degrees at 370 miles an hour is enough to cool you. I had straightened out to prevent unconsciousness, streaking upside down over the top of the bomber. I'd missed the target completely and the top rear gunner figuratively had blasted me from the sky.

This is the heart-breaking thing about combat. Your aircraft is perfectly capable of taking any strain to bring you onto your target, but the human being piloting it isn't. In a dogfight between two fighter pilots this is where physical strength comes in. The stronger pilot can stand sharper turns and thus can outmaneuver the other.

I went into a dive gradually, this time, and came up under the bomber for a belly attack. I must have ripped him plenty with "camera bullets" for he wasn't looking for me to come from underneath.

Ten more times we made beam attacks and ten times I blacked out. I was getting used to the sensation and got over the apprehension of it.

The C.O. next ordered head-on and quarter attacks. These were comparatively easy—at least so far as physical strain. We came head-on for the bombers, firing when in range, pulling up just before a collision and dusting off their backs as we whipped over them.

Then we'd come around for a quarter attack; in this maneuver you slant in from the rear and side, trying to come in where the gunner can't get you by picking one of his "blind spots." Most bombers have "blind spots" not protected by the sweep of their guns. We began varying the head-on and quarter procedure with some sweeps from below up to the bellies of the Hampdens.

There was no attempt to reform our sections now.

[138]

We'd just make an attack individually, circle away, then come in again. There were aircraft all over the sky. It's a wonder there weren't any collisions.

I made one head-on drive for a Hampden, skimming over her so close that the pilot pulled her down in a hurry. Another Hampden broke formation and wheeled away, then another. The bomber pilots were getting a little worried.

This served only to egg us on. We gave them a few close brushes and the entire formation broke up, spreading out over the sky and headed for home. We kept after them. The bombers looked like big birds with swift dragonflies swarming around them. It was a great show. I didn't take time out to admire it, however, for three of us had selected a Hampden and were worrying the life out of him. The gunners in the bomber were good sports for I could see them aiming at us with their cameras.

Finally the bomber pilot brought his aircraft down to within 500 feet of the ground and turned on some speed. The three of us couldn't make beam or belly attacks now, so we confined our activities to head-on and quarter assaults.

We followed the bomber to its own airdrome then called for a vector home. We came into our airdrome and landed. When I climbed from the Hurricane, I

[139]

felt weak and limp, just as if I'd put in an hour of intense combat.

"I guess we brought down all the bombers today, sir," I said to the C.O. as he stood watching some of the other boys come in and land.

"Yes," he drawled. "And I wonder how many times the bombers brought you down. It's a lark when it's a game."

Chapter VIII

INTO THE NIGHT

ONE night after we had been relieved from readiness Shorty and I visited an operations room. We wanted to see how the highly trained aviation experts traced the flights of enemy aircraft and directed British planes to them.

At the concrete entrance to the underground station two sentries, whom we knew, flashed lights on our faces. Recognizing us, they motioned us to a registration book, which we signed.

Descending a long flight of concrete steps, my head just missed a shallow, dimly illuminated ceiling, also of concrete. At the bottom of the steps we opened a door into a large, two-story, brightly lighted circular room. It was bomb-proof, protected by many feet of reinforced concrete overhead. A wide gallery with a railing extended most of the way around it. Below, on the main floor and laid out across a table was a

[141]

huge map of eastern England, the English Channel, the North Sea and the coast of the continent. Uniformed girl plotters of the Woman's Auxiliary Air Force stood about the table, holding what at first looked like long billiard cues. Actually the "cues" were sticks the girls used to move little cards, representing airplanes, across the map. All the girls, or "Waafs" as we called them because of the initials of their service, wore headphones. R.A.F. officers operated the control unit; a squadron leader was in command.

This operations room, similar to those scattered throughout England, was in direct contact with listening posts that detected and reported the movements of enemy aircraft, and the British airdromes, where aircraft could be ordered aloft to intercept the enemy. Operations also was in contact constantly with the British aircraft while they were aloft and was able accurately to plot their courses on the map.

The listening posts were equipped with sound detectors so sensitive that the motor noises of Nazi aircraft could be picked up as they left their bases across the Channel and the North Sea. The "listeners," or crew, used field glasses in addition to the detectors and did an equally accurate job at night as by day, in storm, sleet or fog. They were so well trained that they could determine by sound the number and altitude of the German aircraft.

Shorty and I proudly inspected one of the blackboards in the operations room that had written on it the names of fellows in our squadron. A different color of chalk was used for each section in the squadron. My particular section, known as Red Section, was written up in red chalk. In the same section at this time were Shorty, Phil Leckrone, Bud Orbison, Luke Allen, Flight Lieutenant B. and Squadron Leader C., the last two being Britishers.

There were separate blackboards for each of the other two fighter squadrons at our airdrome. On yet another blackboard the prevailing weather conditions were listed.

"Gentlemen," one of the officers addressed us, "a raid is developing. Would you like to watch it?"

We were standing on the balcony and he motioned to the map. We leaned on the rail and looked down.

"See those cards the girls are pushing across the Channel?" he asked. "Those represent three formations of Nazi bombers converging on Hull."

He explained that each of the three cards which stood on a triangular wooden base represented a formation of Nazi aircraft. Each card was marked with the number of bombers and their approximate altitude. Three girls were moving the cards slowly across the North Sea on the map.

Four other girls moved to the map and placed miniature aircraft on points where I knew night interceptor squadrons were located. One was on our airdrome, which meant the Defiant boys were going up for the show. Two more Waafs were moving miniature planes toward the North Sea. These would be the regular British night patrols.

Shortly one girl began moving the plane that had been on our airdrome. Our Defiants were air-borne! An officer told us two sections of our Defiant boys were going up.

Fascinatedly we watched as one after the other of the tiny planes—each representing at least a section— began moving in on the Nazis.

"How many Jerry bombers in the attack?" Shorty asked.

An officer answered that there were about twenty.

The British sections were just over the coast as the Nazis passed the center of the North Sea. We were told the Germans were flying at about 18,000 feet. There was no moonlight to speak of, so the night fighters would have to get astern of the bombers to see them, the only means of detecting them being their blue-white exhaust trails. When the Defiant boys got within 100 yards they could see the dim outlines of the German planes. These fellows had developed uncanny eyesight for night work by wearing dark glasses during the day and eating a somewhat specialized diet.

Just as if it were an actual battle we were watching, and in a very real sense it was, we saw two British sections reach and touch the foremost Nazi bomber formation. Operations had done its work well and now it was up to the interceptors to make contact with the bombers in the darkness. Of course, if there were clouds, this would be very difficult. However, the weather chart showed only small, scattered patches of clouds in that area.

Shorty and I concentrated on the progress of our Defiant boys. Once they were ordered to change their course northward. Evidently they were being directed at the second bomber formation. The two units finally made contact just east of the Humber River's mouth, a few miles from Hull.

B Controller, a big, hearty officer, put his hand over a microphone long enough to grin at us, "Two tallyho's already. That means trouble for one Jerry formation!"

"Tallyho," of course, is the R.A.F. battle cry. In this case it meant that two Defiants had spotted and were attacking the bombers. For a moment B Controller was through giving directions. Once the enemy was contacted, he had to wait until a call came from one of the fighter pilots for a vector home or for more directions to continue the fight. After the attack, the British interceptors would have to be brought home separately, for they would lose each other in the dark.

One little card was nearly over Hull and we knew that at least part of a bomber formation had broken through. The one attacked by our Defiants was moving away from the coast! The Defiants evidently had broken it up or had downed its leader. The third German formation was over the coast south of the Humber and moving inland. It had been intercepted once by the night patrols, but evidently had gotten through, perhaps under cover of clouds.

Shorty's usually jovial face was drawn and tense as he watched the map.

Orders came to the operations room to call off the fighters. Hull was going to turn on the searchlights and open up with archies. The Waafs, as soon as they learned that there were six Defiants from our airdrome in the fight, placed six small aircraft on the map. The boys were being vectored home. We were elated to see that there were no casualties.

Night fighting at this period of the war was tough and sometimes discouraging. It was just before the days of the infrared screen, that marvelous night-fighting tool. With its aid the British increased the night fatalities of the Jerries alarmingly. The screen is attached to the aircraft's dashboard and through it the enemy actually can be seen, no matter how dark the night or how thick the clouds. Its use was made possible because aircraft motors radiate infrared waves. These waves light up the aircraft with "invisible light"—invisible, that is, to the unaided eye. The screen picks up this light.

As the second of the three cards reached Hull on the map, Shorty turned to me and said: "Hell, Jack, we ought to be up there giving those Jerries a few rounds of lead. Let's get out of here!"

I knew how he felt. We hurried out, signing the register again as we reached the top of the stairs. Outside it was dark and quiet—at least where we were.

The next morning broke blustery and cold. "Typical early November weather," my batman described it. We filed into the dispersal hut after checking our aircraft in the cutting, damp air. American and British pilots alike reflected the frowning sky's mood. It wasn't so much the weather that made us feel this way, it was the fact Jerry had become very shy of the daylight. That meant there would be little flying to do and flying is the champagne without which a pilot begins to lose the buoyancy that only altitude and a stout aircraft can give him.

The one thing that bucked us up was that during the night our Defiant fighter boys had knocked down two Dornier 215's without a single loss to themselves. They were having all the luck!

Some dozen of us, mostly Americans, gathered around the fireplace, the only cheerful thing in the hut. Shorty was telling the C.O. of our visit to the operations room, emphasizing how tough it made us feel, not to be up there having a crack at the Jerries.

"I'm glad you chaps feel that way," the C.O. said, "because tomorrow the Eagle Squadron starts training for night patrol."

He looked from one to the other of us, enjoying the way our faces abruptly lost their glumness. Then he added, "I take it you're interested. Report in readiness tomorrow noon. Take tomorrow morning off and get some extra sleep. For once, you'll need your wits about you at night."

That noon at lunch, for the first time in my life, I almost enjoyed eating brussels sprouts. I took an overdose of pills we always had on the table at meals.

The pills, piled on a plate, were guarded by a small sign which read: "For night-flying personnel only," and contained concentrated vitamin A.

That night we stayed up late so we could sleep in the morning. Some of us wandered over to the pub in a near-by town for a nightcap before turning in. We ran into three Americans who were coming to the station the next day to see us. They'd arrived late so were going to stop overnight at a hotel.

They were ferry pilots who transported bombers from factories in Britain to various airdromes. One of them, E. O., a famous American racing pilot, seemed surprised that we were in a fighter unit after we told him we were getting about ninety dollars a month, out of which we paid room, board, and a small income tax. He said there was a lot more money in ferrying planes. We told him that we didn't come over here to make money, that we wanted to fight.

"Yes," I emphasized, "we had a Nazi prisoner call us screwy for wanting to fight, so I guess it's all right if you call us that, too."

It was no hardship at all, sleeping several hours after dawn, I discovered the next morning. When I awoke it was broad daylight. Luke was still sawing wood. I aroused him and we dressed, then went down to breakfast. Bud, Shorty, and Kolendorski were at the table when we arrived. Some of the others already had breakfasted and left. We ate leisurely, reading the London morning papers, which always were ready for us when we got up.

After breakfast the five of us inspected our aircraft with extra thoroughness. I climbed onto the wide, camouflaged wing and crawled into the deep cockpit. I opened the oxygen valves to check the gauge. We probably wouldn't need oxygen for the first night hop, but you never could be sure. Making certain the pressure was up in the air pipes for the landing gear, I then checked the petrol and oil supply and noticed by the motor temperature gauge that the engine had been warmed up by my mechanic.

The mechanic and armorer came over to see how I was getting on and we started up the motor. While they lay on the tail, I revved up the Merlin several times. She was working beautifully. Then, with the motor idling, I flipped the radio key to send and called operations. I got a response and informed them I was just testing. Above all, I'd need the radio. If you get lost at night you're a gone goose if your radio doesn't function!

Finally the gunsight was checked; this was something else that might come in handy. I didn't bring the parachute out to lay on the wing as was my custom because there was moisture in the air. Moisture doesn't do a 'chute any good, Shorty had emphasized. The routine check finally done, I switched off the motor and signed on duty for the rest of the day.

The only activity that afternoon was tea, consisting of bread, cookies and, of course, tea, and a hearty supper of rabbit, potatoes, the inevitable brussels sprouts, coffee and a dessert of cheese.

We finished dinner quickly to hustle back to the dispersal hut. The C.O. said that Luke, Bud and I were to be the first three to make the night hop. We were to take off at fifteen-second intervals, circle the field in a flight pattern and land. We strapped on our 'chutes and hurried out, catching the C.O.'s final words, "Believe your instruments, boys. There's nothing else you can safely believe in at night!"

Pilots from all three squadrons who were not on night duty were on the 'drome's apron to watch proceedings. The C.O. took a portable radio and climbed to the watch office; he was going to be our "operations," using the code name of "Locust Control." I was assigned my old numbers, two, zero, with the prefix "Rinzo."

Except for obstruction lights on buildings, the taxiing post at the end of the field and a row of dim lights, called the flare path, extending down the runway, the airdrome was dark.

We trotted across to our aircraft, which had been

pushed from their dispersal bays. All the boys in my ground crew were by my Hurricane; they were going to be certain that I made a perfect landing in the dark.

"You'll make a perfect hop of it, sir," my mechanic assured me.

"Thanks, Triggs," I nodded as I stepped on the wing, "I reckon eagles can be converted into owls."

The motor already was turning over. I slid into the seat, prepared for the take-off, and looked at the watchtower. The green light flashed at me, indicating I was to take off first.

I taxied onto the runway, swinging her fuselage parallel to the flare path. With a salute to the boys holding the wings, I gunned her. Not being able to see the ground, I watched the flare path lights as they started sliding by, faster and faster.

Just before reaching the last light, I took off into the blackness. Then the only light I could see was the reassuring glow of the instruments on the dash panel. Instinctively, I wanted to glance back at the flare path to be sure I was climbing correctly, but I knew this might be as fatal a move as Lot's wife made when she looked back and was turned into a pillar of salt. Many pilots have been killed looking around on a night take-off. Just as I discovered in that first fog hop, this tends to make the aircraft turn with you and at the low take-off speed such a turn easily could cause a quick spin into the deck. So I kept my eyes on the instruments, imagining them to be the landscape by which I could orient my flight. Actually they were.

I climbed straight to 1,000 feet, then watched the directional gyro in making a 180-degree turn.

Then I looked out. Below and ahead was the flare path. As I passed over the airdrome I tapped out the letters of the day in Morse code, indicating I was a friendly aircraft. The letters were flashed from an amber light located under the tail assembly and could be seen from the ground.

In the air by yourself at night, you certainly get an "all alone" feeling. Except for the dim flare path, everything was in darkness. All England was under continuous blackout.

Making a complete circle of the airdrome, I began a power glide, lowering flaps and undercarriage for a landing. When the flaps are down, you can feel the aircraft lift a little, settle back and slow down. A green light flashed from the watchtower, so I brought her low over where I thought the field boundary was located. It was tough, coming in at 100 miles an hour with nothing to gauge where the surface of the field was except a long row of lights that didn't illuminate any of the ground around it.

About fifteen feet above where the landing strip must be, I spotted an amber light. It was moving slightly and couldn't be far from me. Suddenly a searchlight flooded the runway with light. A scant 100 feet ahead and just taking off was a coal black Defiant fighter. Evidently its pilot had received a scramble call.

Although both of us were headed into the wind, I was gaining on him rapidly! So I gunned the motor, retracted the undercarriage and pulled up and to the side of the plane. I had almost piled into him! I gained speed and altitude fast and rounded the airdrome again, hoping I wouldn't pile into the tail of either Bud or Luke. Over the radio I could hear the C.O.'s voice directing them out of the way.

I came down the second time and again the floodlight was turned on just before the wheels grated the runway. As soon as they touched, the floodlight was extinguished. Somehow I made just about a perfect three-point landing.

As I taxied up the runway the radio crackled and a voice called, "Hello. This is Locust Control. Who just landed? Who was that?"

Flipping the radio key to send I answered, "Hello,

Locust Control. This is Rinzo Two Zero. Rinzo Two Zero just landed."

"Very good. Very good, Rinzo Two Zero. Try it again."

I made three more take-offs and landings and presume Bud and Luke did the same. As I descended for the fifth one, flaps and undercarriage down, the flare path lights suddenly were extinguished! This must be part of the test, I decided, and came lower, losing speed all the time. If I had to land in total darkness, I wanted to hit the ground as easily as possible.

"Hello, Rinzo Hurricane test pilots!" came the C.O.'s voice. He sounded excited. "Bandits in vicinity. Remain air-borne and orbit."

Orbit meant to fly in a circle. Quickly I gunned her; I didn't dare pull up the undercarriage yet, for the aircraft was only a few feet from the ground and might touch the turf any moment. I felt her touch, but she was accelerating rapidly and I was able to lift her off quickly because the flaps were down. You can take off the ground in a hurry if you use a little flap.

Up I went, wishing the C.O. would vector us onto the Jerries. But he didn't and I made four slow circles before I was ordered down—in the darkness. The Hurricane started settling. The C.O. ordered me to keep coming down, adding that lights would be turned on just before I hit. I hoped so! I tried to keep her speed back. Just as the controls began getting mushy, indicating the aircraft was near a stall, the flare path lights pin-pointed the blackness about a dozen feet below. The second my wheels felt the turf, the lights went out. The landing was all right except that I nearly rammed into the T-shaped taxiing post. This post mounted several small electric bulbs which were made invisible from above by visors cut from tin cans. It was used as a guide in landing and I stopped just two feet from it!

This marked the beginning of intensive night training. We did this in addition to a full day in readiness in the hut.

Chapter IX

SWASTIKA TARGETS

THE first night we got leave from night training, Andy Mamedoff, Phil Leckrone and I took a trip to a famous hotel in Lincolnshire to attend a formal dance. It wasn't so much the dance that attracted us, but the prospect of meeting some famous British pilots who were planning to be there.

We arrived a little early, just before the orchestra started up, so we wandered into a side room. Two British pilots, one a husky blond and the other a slender, dark fellow, rose as we entered and introduced themselves. They needed no introduction, for we had heard a great deal about them. The blond was Flight Lieutenant R. A. B. Learoyd, V.C., and his companion Flight Lieutenant J. B. Nicolson, V.C. The V.C., of course, meant that they had been decorated with the Victoria Cross.

We chatted awhile about flying in general until

five more British pilots came in. We Americans told the others we hadn't seen any action yet, although we hoped to any day, and were interested in first-hand accounts of aerial combats. At first the Britishers were reticent about describing their adventures. After I emphasized that knowing something of their experiences would help us in combat, they began to thaw out. The music started in the ballroom, but the ten of us had started "hangar flying" so weren't very interested in dancing at the moment.

I wish I could give you the names of the pilots who took part in some of the flights we heard described. They deserve all the credit coming to them, but regulations forbid revealing who they were.

One of the fighter pilots recounted how, while he was dogfighting one Jerry over England, another one —an Me. 109—got on his tail. He got the Nazi he was after, but the one chasing him shot an incendiary bullet or a cannon shell into his instrument panel, setting it afire. Almost at the same instant a heavy caliber machine-gun bullet ripped through the calf of one leg.

The first gush of flame and smoke blinding him for a moment, he went into a steep dive. He slid back the hatch and unfastened his Sutton harness so he could bail out. The rush of air through the open hatch cleared the smoke from his greenhouse, and he saw below him an Me. 110, a twin-motored combination fighter and light bomber.

Although flames were searing his control stick with blow-torch intensity, the Britisher grabbed it with his mittened right hand and steered his Spitfire for the Me. When within range, he pressed the firing button. While the fire cooked his right hand, even through the heavy mitten and silk glove, to the stick handle, he kept on shooting. Finally the Messerschmitt fell away into a tailspin and crashed.

To get loose from the stick, the Britisher had to grab his right wrist with his left hand and jerk his hand loose, pulling off three fingers! He jumped from his flaming aircraft and when a safe distance from it, pulled the ripcord, opening his parachute.

About 200 feet from the ground he saw an elderly Englishman in civilian clothes—a member of the home guard—aiming a shotgun up at him. The pilot yelled and waved. This was the time when many English people were certain Hitler was going to try a parachute troop invasion, and the home guardsman apparently was convinced his target was a paratrooper.

He let go with two barrels. The wounded pilot was able to turn his face away in time and received the buckshot in his back and legs. The shot penetrated his heavy flying suit in several places, wounding him severely. It was lucky his parachute wasn't ripped to pieces.

When he landed and it was discovered he was an R.A.F. pilot, several townspeople nearly mobbed the shocked home guardsman. Troops arrived in time to save him from harm. Recovering after a brief hospital stay, the pilot was decorated for his heroism; King George himself presented the coveted medal.

A distinguished bomber pilot described a daylight assault on a canal in Holland through which Nazis were pouring supplies to the coast for a possible invasion of Britain. There was great need to put the canal out of service quickly. The assignment was entirely outside the line of duty because the attack had to be made in broad daylight by one aircraft. Owing to the extreme risk involved, a call was made for volunteers. This pilot responded and was accepted.

He was told he would have no fighter plane escort because a convoy of fighters would attract the enemy's attention and probably make the attack unsuccessful. The element of surprise was vital.

The pilot and his crew, who was as anxious for the assignment as he, took off in the early morning, sneaked safely over the Channel and reached the target. A barge was being taken through the canal. The pilot made a run over the target at an altitude of 500 feet. He wanted to make sure the barge was hit. Machine-guns from the barge and along the shore blazed at him. He came back low, well within machine-gun range, and dumped his full load of bombs on the barge. It blew up and blocked the canal. Then he and his crew made their escape.

Two other British pilots came in to join the discussion. One was the sergeant pilot of a bomber that had taken part in raids on Norwegian invasion bases. He described a trip, which was calm enough on the way over and during the actual bombing. However, on the return leg the squadron ran into a pea-soup fog. His bomber ran out of petrol after he had flown it around waiting for the heavy mist to clear a bit. He brought the plane down on the sea, believing it to be land. Fortunately they landed close to the beach and all hands managed to get ashore. Several other bombers of the formation also failed to reach their bases. Some crash-landed. The crews of others bailed out. All the bombers had been in the air at least five hours.

Speaking of hours in the air, British pilots had the greatest respect for American Consolidated Catalina patrol bombers. It was in one of these long-range ships that Britishers later spotted the German battle-ship *Bismarck*, thus making it possible to torpedo and sink her. These Consolidateds were able to stay aloft as long as thirty hours before refueling. They did yeoman duty in driving the submarines far from Britain's shores. Sub crews, of course, live in deadly fear of planes. One patrol bomber pilot told us he could spot a sub from the air when the submersible was fifty feet below the water's surface. When an air-craft is directly over a submarine, there is no reflec-tion from the surface of the sea and the pilot can peer far down into the water. From a ship this would be impossible.

A fighter pilot from the north of England told us how a Junkers 88 came in low over his 'drome in broad daylight. Guns were trained on the plane, but as its flaps and wheels were down the gunners with-held their fire. They were on the alert, however, be-cause Nazi bombers had been known to glide down toward British 'dromes with flaps and wheels down as if they'd surrendered and were about to land. Then, when over the 'drome, they would drop their bombs and roar away.

As the plane landed, the British troops ran out to capture the crew. Each of the four Germans who crawled out of the plane carried a suitcase. The Nazis explained to their captors that they had run out of petrol. Asked to explain their suitcases, they replied that they and other bomber crews had been taking off from French airdromes, coming over England to dump their loads, then heading back to Norwegian bases. Then they'd take off from Norway, come to England and return to France. Thus they had to carry many of their belongings with them. We figured that because the Nazis didn't want to let their airmen know of their losses, they kept shifting them, as they did these fellows, from one airdrome to another.

Another bomber pilot described a night raid on Berlin. He said he had never seen such an antiaircraft barrage as met the British as they roared over the outskirts of the German capital. It was like an enormous white fountain of fire with a wide base and closing, pyramid-shaped, at the top. Shells were bursting at many altitudes. Unsuccessfully, the bombers, all Blenheims, tried to climb above the blasts.

The target was a factory in the heart of Berlin and, the pilot said, the Britishers spent fifty-five minutes cruising through the explosive hell looking for it. Finally, aided by light from bursting shells and flares dropped by British planes, the telltale smokestacks were spotted.

[163]

After the pilot had dropped all but one of his bombs, a shell burst near by, the concussion tossing the bomber upside down and hurling several shell fragments through the fuselage and one wing. The crew thought they were goners as the aircraft lost several thousand feet in altitude. At the last moment the pilot managed to right his ship. A big chunk of steel had ripped through the undercarriage, forcing the pilot, when he arrived at his home airdrome, to belly-land.

Other adventures were told in that hotel room. In most of them the element of heroism under fire played a striking part. But the pilots considered that what they had done was merely part of the job. They all believed that their job was something that had to be done well, regardless of the cost to themselves. While we learned something about flying, we learned more about the sacredness of devotion to duty.

Chapter X

COVENTRY

"ARMISTICE DAY is only hazily remembered here. We are now fighting for the greatest armistice in history. One that will last longer than twenty years."

As I finished this last paragraph of a letter to my mother, the C.O. entered the dispersal hut. I noticed by the early dawn light that his face was white and lined. Jerry had been coming over hot and heavy the past few nights and I thought this might be what was worrying him.

"Up late last night, sir?" I asked.

He nodded and sat down beside me. "I'm a bit fagged, Jack. Been doing a little night patrol."

That explained the somber, tired look we had noticed on his face for several days. Not only had he been doing his daily trick with us, he had been making night patrols by himself after we had finished our night practice and gone to bed. In other words, he was on duty nearly around the clock.

Bud Orbison overheard the conversation and came over.

"I'd like to volunteer for night patrol with you, sir," he said.

Several of us volunteered before the C.O. could answer. When he did, it was to say, "All right, boys, you make your first patrol tomorrow night."

That meant we were to come on duty at noon, stay in readiness for a scramble call or possible daylight patrol until dark, then make a night patrol.

The first night, six of us went up. Under a waxing moon, I patrolled Manchester, that large city being so completely blacked out it was indistinguishable from the rest of the countryside, even by moonlight. I had no time, however, to peer at the landscape many thousand feet below. Directed by radio in a great, sweeping circle over the city, I looked and looked into the dim night for the blue-white flare of a Nazi bomber's exhaust. I saw none. Constantly staring into the darkness for a Jerry kept away an unusual sensation of loneliness that crept upon me. It was a feeling that I was a lone human being in space, and that the world I had known was ages away.

Several nights later the C.O., Andy, Bud, Luke and I were playing poker in the hut. We hadn't gone up on patrol. The C.O. had kept us grounded be-

[166]

cause, he said, "something important might develop."

He interrupted the game every few minutes to talk over the French field phone to operations. Then he would use the box phone to instruct the mechanics to keep our aircraft warmed up. We occasionally heard a "cough, cough" and "brrrrrup" as a crew started up a motor.

Suddenly over the Tannoy loud-speaker came the command:

"Night-flying pilots come to readiness! Come to readiness!"

The C.O. jumped from his chair and grabbed the field phone. We crowded around him.

"Yes," he was saying, "Coventry. We're in readiness now. Fifteen minutes. Check."

He hung up the phone. "Be ready to take off in fifteen minutes at ten-second intervals. We're patrolling Coventry. Big flap developing."

Big flap meant a big raid! And we were to get a crack at the Nazis. As the four of us reached for our parachutes, the C.O. warned, "Take it easy, boys. We have to wait in the hut fifteen minutes to get final orders. Let's finish our game."

It was no time for poker, but the C.O. wanted to keep the four of us from getting nervous. Tenseness resulting from this slows muscular reactions. Fifteen minutes later, right on the nose, we got telephonic confirmation to take off immediately.

Wearing fur-lined Irving suits because it was very cold, we helped each other with our parachutes and ran out into the darkness. Every light on the airdrome was turned off. There were a few scattered clouds, but not enough completely to hide the landscape, which was painted with the bluish light of a full moon.

"Thumbs up, boys. We'll get a crack at 'em to-night," called the C.O. as he left our running group for his aircraft. All the planes were on the line, ready to take off.

I jumped onto the wing of my Hurricane and climbed into the cockpit, flipping on the dash lights. Fastening the Sutton harness, plugging in the radio and oxygen tubes and snapping the oxygen mask in place across my face, I turned the electric starter switch, yelling, "Contact!" The motor burst into noisy life. Quickly I closed the hatch and pulled on silk gloves and flying mittens as my electrician wheeled away the portable batteries that were plugged into the Hurricane's belly to power the self-starter.

The corporal of the flare path flashed a green light at the C.O. Immediately his motor roared and his

[168]

Hurricane swung out onto the runway. I could see the undulating flash of his exhaust. As he lined up into the wind, the flare path lights were switched on. Tail up, the C.O.'s Hurricane roared off into the night.

I counted ten seconds on my watch. Then Luke roared out and took off. Ten more seconds. I pushed the throttle and taxied to the starting mark. Two members of my crew shoved the wings at right angles to the wind, then gave me a thumbs up salute. I responded and thundered down the runway. Nearing the last light I pulled her off the turf. I heard Luke informing operations, or Locust Control, he was airborne. Moving the undercarriage lever, I heard a thump as the wheels folded inward and reached their retracted position. The powerful aircraft picked up climbing speed the instant the wheels were up. The flare path lights must have been on about thirty seconds now and I hoped there were no Nazi bombers lurking about. The lights would make a perfect target.

Flipping the radio key to send, I called: "Hello, Locust Control. Rinzo Two Zero calling. Are you receiving me?"

"Hello, Rinzo Two Zero," came the answer, "receiving you loud and clear. Over."

"Hello, Locust Control. Rinzo Two Zero airborne. Over."

"Hello, Rinzo Two Zero. Locust Control answering. Understand you are air-borne. Listening out."

The radio was quiet for several seconds until operations gave the C.O. and Luke a vector. As I climbed steadily, waiting for directions, I heard Bud and Andy report they were air-borne. My eyes roved over the instruments. I was trying to check them all to keep from feeling a bit nervous. As the altimeter needle touched the 500-foot mark, I changed the prop pitch to 2,600 R.P.M. so the motor wouldn't turn over so fast. At 1,000 feet I banked into a 180-degree, one needle-width level turn. Somewhere ahead in the blue blackness were the C.O. and Luke. Behind were Bud and Andy. By following prearranged navigation plans precisely we would all reach the same objective and without any danger of a collision.

The radio crackled in the earphones and operations called me; I answered that I was receiving operations "strength nina." "Nina" meant nine but was more easily understood over the R.T. Strength nine meant reception was strong. Operations ordered me to "vector two, one, five. Angels twelve." The orders were to set the gyro compass at 215 and to climb to 12,000 feet.

In a gradual climb, I reached 12,000 in about three minutes. Glancing out the hatch, I could see nothing below but the bluish blackness of moonlight reflecting on a slight haze. I hoped we could spot the Jerries in this semi-illumination. It was a strange sensation, I thought as more minutes passed, being on the way to protect an invisible city against an unseen foe. Little did I know I was going to witness one of the most devastating bombing raids in the history of warfare.

My knees got cold above my boots in this high altitude and I slapped them vigorously to stir up circulation. The radio began to give off mutterings. It wasn't static, but some sort of mumbling conversation. I tried to catch it but couldn't. It might be a German controller on nearly the same wave length as ours talking to his planes.

Finally the mumbling was drowned by the C.O.'s voice:

"Tallyhoooo!"

Somewhere a little more than a mile ahead the C.O. was attacking a Jerry! Happy hunting, Rinzo Three Nine! Ahead in the darkness was a tiny streak of light, like a dim shooting star, moving across and down in front of me. It must be the C.O.'s tracer bullets as he followed his target. Over the R.T. came a faint muttering that might be his machine guns. The light blacked out, only to resume again. For an instant, I caught the glint of a wing in the moonlight. A ruddy streak appeared, at first descending in a slant, then falling directly earthward and disappearing. One of the planes in that scrap was downed!

I listened anxiously for the C.O.'s voice on the R.T. All I heard was operations telling Luke to climb higher. Had the C.O. been shot down?

"Hello, Rinzo Two Zero. Locust Control calling," operations' voice crackled. "Are you receiving me?"

"Hello, Locust Control. Rinzo Two Zero answering. Receiving you strength six. Over."

Operations answered by ordering me up another thousand feet. "Ops'" voice was fainter, about strength six. This was natural because I was moving away from the station. If reception dropped to strength two or three, operations would switch me to a closer station. If the nearer station's reception wasn't louder it meant the radio was failing and I'd have to be vectored to an airdrome in a hurry.

I flew for five more minutes in the great, lonely well of night. The only object I could see distinctly was the round moon. Operations called once to vector me still higher. I turned on the oxygen and took several satisfying inhalations of the stuff. Then again the radio crackled to life and operations' voice came over the earphones:

"Rinzo Two Zero. Locust Control calling. Orbit. Objective."

I was over Coventry already! Banking into a wide turn I looked below. Aside from a few light and scattered clouds, reflecting a wraithlike bluish glow of the moon, I could see nothing. To the east searchlight beams moved slowly in the sky.

A welcome sound came over the R.T. It was the C.O., calling operations for a vector. I was much relieved to know he was still in the sky. I wanted to ask him what had happened, but of course I couldn't. The R.T. had to be clear for sudden orders.

I'd set a course for a circle of several miles' radius over the objective when I heard Andy and then Bud receive instructions to orbit. Now the five of us must be over the objective, not all flying at the same altitude, however. We weren't the only interceptors aloft; there must be many others from other airdromes. Their radio wave lengths were different from ours, so we didn't interfere with their conversations.

Suddenly far below a tiny orange light appeared. Then another. They were stationary so they must be on the ground. As I looked, several more winked on,

[173]

a considerable distance from the first ones. They were fires starting from incendiary bombs. As others became visible, the first one went out. Then the second disappeared. But for every one that was extinguished, five blossomed in the night. They looked innocent enough from this altitude, like fireflies at rest on a lawn. The fire watchers and wardens who were fighting them, probably had a far different impression.

A wider and wider area was being sown with the fast-growing seeds of destruction. Several of the spots spread and blended into others and soon in the place of pin-point fires there were gigantic infernos. The Nazis must be coming over by the score, using the thin cloud wisps below as a cover. The rapidly increasing reddish light from the fires made the clouds glow dully at the edges.

Then, several thousand feet below and silhouetted against the glow of the fires, I spotted a winged object skulking through a cloud. It was a twin-engined Nazi bomber! It had large bat-wings, the "bites" or inward curves on the trailing edges of the wings where they joined the fuselage marked it as a Heinkel 111.

Luckily I had set my gunsights for the seventy-five-foot wing span of a Heinkel. Here was my chance! My right hand trembled as I snapped on the sights and turned the firing button guard to "fire" position. Quick, before the Heinkel disappeared beyond the fire! Sucking in deep breaths of oxygen through dry lips, I put her into a dive. It would be a quarter attack. The Hurricane roared down, then leveled off in the thin mist.

Where was the Heinkel? There! Just ahead. The Hurricane caught up with the racing silhouette. But it was transparent! Holy thunder! I was attacking the shadow of a bomber that was flying somewhere below the cloud! If any of the fellows had heard about this they'd call me Pilot Officer Don Quixote! The only good thing was that, in the excitement of expected battle, I'd forgotten to shout "Tallyho."

The Hurricane swept under the cloud and began rocking a little. The fires below were creating a strong thermal of rising warm air, making the atmosphere rough. I couldn't see the Heinkel so I took a squint below. Miniature cars, probably ambulances, and fire trucks, brightly lighted by a dozen fires, were crawling through streets that must be furnaces! Almost directly below were four flashes of light, tossing up undulating billows of smoke. The Jerries were beginning to drop explosives.

Looking up I caught sight of three Heinkels skimming in a vic just inside the clouds. They weren't shadows, either. There were crosses on the under-side of their wings. I yelled "Tallyhoo!" as the Hurricane vaulted upstairs to make a belly attack on the bomber to my left. Just before I got within range, the big aircraft dropped a stick of bombs and pulled up into the cloud. I was so anxious to get him I went up into it, too, although I knew I probably couldn't spot him quickly enough among the shadowy cloud mists to get in a long burst. My heart was thumping almost as loudly as the motor.

The mist came down to meet me and I caught sight of something dark that might have been the black belly of a bomber. For the first time in my life I pressed the firing button. The stick vibrated a bit and I heard through my helmet a long "brrrrrrrrruuuup" as bullets shot from the eight machine guns. White tracer streaks disappeared into the black object, which slid past me directly overhead.

Had I maneuvered to follow him I would have blacked out, so I went on up through the cloud, the Hurricane's wings emitting a screaming whistle. The protecting flaps over the gun ports, put on to lessen air resistance, were shot away and the wind, passing by at about 250 miles an hour, was whistling in the gun barrels. I'd had my first crack at the enemy.

Near the illuminated edge of a cloud the enlarged

shadows of four more bombers flashed by, going in the opposite direction from me. The Nazis must be sending them over by the hundreds tonight. Although the fires and moonlight made aircraft plainly visible in certain areas, the small clouds and smoke caused the trickiest shadows. It was a weird sensation, stalking the enemy and his huge reflections.

I returned to my assigned level and resumed patrol. Unfortunately, now it was all too easy to circle the objective. Great fires were raging below. I thought of the many women and children who must be suffering from this inhuman devastation. Another "Tallyhoo!" over the R.T. cheered me up a little. I couldn't recognize the voice, but one of the boys in the squadron was making an attack. There was more R.T. conversation. I didn't pay much attention to it for I was too busy trying to spot another Nazi.

There was a great flash of light somewhere in a cloud beneath me. That meant a bomber had exploded. Perhaps it was the result of the "Tallyho" I'd just heard.

As the Hurricane rounded the east side of the city and headed west I sighted an aircraft, the under side of which was etched in red. It was traveling in the same direction as I, and was about 500 yards in front. The black aircraft ahead appeared to be smaller and looked like a British Blenheim I. There were no Blenheims up here and the only Nazi bomber that looked like them was the Junkers 88. This must be one of them. Since its wing span was fifteen feet less than a Heinkel, I corrected the gunsight.

Slanting down to ride in on his tail, the Hurricane began closing in a bit too fast. Not wanting to overshoot him, I lowered the flaps a little and eased off the throttle. My thumb was tense against the trigger button and I had to concentrate to keep from firing too soon. If the Jerry saw me, he could dive for a cloud. The oxygen felt cold against my face where it slipped out the side of the mask. Steady! I squinted into the sights, which glowed dull red, and kept a bead on the Jerry. Apparently I hadn't been spotted yet as the Junkers streaked straight ahead at about 280 miles an hour, rising and falling in the heat-roughened air. Once the Hurricane jumped around as it got in his propeller blast. I climbed above it.

"Tallyho!" I yelled throatily into the mike, hoping the radio key was on send. It was too late to find out now. I had to keep one hand on the firing button and the other on the throttle.

His wing tips touched each side of the sight ring. He was within range! My thumb pressed the firing button. The Hurricane slowed from the recoil and I

[178]

gave her a little throttle. Snaky streaks of white from the tracers reached from my wing into the tail of the Junkers.

The Jerry banked slightly and I glanced through the windscreen to see that he didn't try to get away. Suddenly blackness enveloped the windscreen. I could see nothing! I blinked and stopped firing. It wasn't my eyesight that was failing because the instrument panel still glowed brightly. I glanced around and saw light coming through the rear part of the glass sliding hatch.

Then I realized what had happened. The Nazis had a trick of throwing out black oil to blind a chasing enemy. Dirty oil was plastered on my windscreen. Had I been an experienced pilot, I wouldn't have sailed calmly up on the tail but would have stayed several feet above.

Pulling up the flaps I gunned her again. The rushing air blew off part of the fuel oil, at least enough so I could see out dimly. The bomber had disappeared.

Climbing to my patrol level, I noticed the windscreen was still badly streaked with oil. I snapped off the gunsight and turned the firing button to "safe," hoping to get one more crack at a Jerry tonight!

The fires below had become so great that I easily

could have read a newspaper in the cockpit from the glare. The air was quite bumpy and warm. Visibility actually was cut by the light, which glanced glaringly off the windscreen. Enormous smoke clouds billowed up from below. Occasionally I passed through one. As I glanced down at this dirty work of the Nazis, there were two huge explosions on the ground, shooting up enormous umbrellas of smoke that gradually stretched upward in great treelike masses. Many seconds later I heard two dull booms over the roar of the motor and shriek of the gun mouths.

Still more explosions dotted the fiery mass below. It must be an enormous raid. The Nazis evidently were coming over in small formations, keeping within the clouds for the most part. I saw three bombers downed, one in flames, one with a wing torn off and a third blown up. The night patrol planes were taking a toll.

The smoke began to thicken and obliterate the fires. Visibility dimmed. It seemed an age since I had come aloft. Smoke crept into the cabin and smarted my eyes as I kept hunting, hunting for the Nazi bomber fleets that were sneaking in to drop their explosives.

The R.T. crackled a vector to the C.O. Then an

order came for Luke, Bud, Andy and me. The patrol was being recalled. Either we were to be replaced or all British aircraft were to be removed so the anti-aircraft guns could open up.

I had to cross over the heart of the fire to get to the base. The Hurricane pitched and bucked in the turbulent air. Suddenly the aircraft rose so quickly I was nearly shoved through the armored seat. Then it banked on its port wing and I had to move fast to keep her from turning over. What was happening?

Just below, black puffs of antiaircraft shells exploded around a Nazi bomber that had popped out of a smoke cloud. Before I could turn and dive on it, a shell exploded under his starboard motor, wrenching it from its nacelle. The Nazi went into a shallow glide. Just before it disappeared into some more smoke its starboard wing buckled upward. That guy wasn't going to do any more bombing in a hurry. It had been concussion from the exploding antiaircraft shells that had nearly upset my Hurricane. The archie gunners below hadn't seen me.

I got out of that hell of fire and smoke as quickly as possible. The petrol was getting low and the oil streaks on the windscreen still interfered with my vision. When I left the red glow of Coventry behind, the moonlit atmosphere seemed unusually peaceful

[181]

and quiet. The sky was clear and the round moon looked down peacefully. It was an almost unbelievable contrast to the ugly night over Coventry, where a Nazi war lord was trying to blast a city off the face of this moonlit land.

After many minutes I got radio instructions: "Pancake! You are over base."

The flare path was turned on and I settled her down for the landing. At this instant a strong crosswind eased the plane dangerously close to the flare path lights. The lines of oil on the windscreen had caused me to misjudge the distances and land too close to the lights. The Hurricane was coming in a little too hot—120 miles an hour—and I saw the corporal of the flare path duck when my starboard wing nearly smacked him on the back. As the wheels hit the ground hard, the Hurricane bounced up about fifty feet. I gave her the throttle a bit and mushed her down. The next time she hit she stayed down and taxied along at 100 miles an hour, barely missing the portable chance light or field searchlight.

I eased on the brakes and she slowed to a stop near the end of the field. Perspiration was oozing out of me as I turned her and taxied to the dispersal bay. My ground crew cheered wildly as the aircraft stopped. They'd heard the wind whistle in the gun ports and knew I'd gotten a crack at a Jerry.

I told them I'd had my first shots at the Nazis but hadn't bagged any aircraft. Inspection of the Hurricane showed a mess of dirty oil over the motor cowling, but no damage. I was glad of that.

Andy and Bud already were back and had asked the C.O. if we couldn't refuel and go up again. He'd shaken his head. The boys said he felt very blue, even though he had knocked down two Heinkels.

Luke came in and landed. None of us could claim victories, although three of us had used our guns. We walked over to the C.O., who had waited on the field until Luke had climbed from his Hurricane. Several other boys from our squadron joined us as we congratulated the C.O. and tried to buck him up.

"Coventry took a hell of a pasting, boys," was all he said as he turned, parachute under his arm, and walked wearily into the office to make out his combat report.

He wasn't to be comforted.

Chapter XI

TOIL AND SWEAT

WHEN we finally piled into bed after the Coventry patrol, I couldn't go to sleep for a long time. And when I did, it was an unrestful slumber, filled with ogrelike pilots releasing bombs with machine-gun rapidity, and enormous fires that covered great, arching sweeps of the earth. As in most nightmares, the elements of this one were enlarged out of all proportion.

I awakened a couple of hours before dawn to find Luke still asleep. Nothing bothered that fellow when it came time to pound his ears. I lay there for nearly an hour. Then, as it was about the time pilots working the morning trick were getting up, I climbed out of bed quietly and dressed in my R.A.F. uniform. Phil Leckrone, Jim McGinnis and I had leave for the day and we were planning a trip down to London.

I met these two boys at breakfast. They were talking earnestly to Andy Mamedoff. I was surprised to see Andy up so early, but soon learned why. He was telling the fellows that his mechanic had a sister in Coventry and hadn't heard from her since the bombing. Neither he nor Andy could get the time off to go down and investigate.

McGinnis greeted me with, "Looks as if we take a trip to Coventry today, Jack."

That was how, soon after dawn, the three of us climbed into an R.A.F. motor lorry and started off on the two-and-a-half-hour trip to Coventry. Not far from our objective we passed through Leicester, where we saw more red brick buildings than I thought existed. We had to travel slowly as we neared the stricken city because there were so many trucks bringing in supplies of all kinds. Smeary towers of smoke guided us the last eight miles. Fires still were burning.

Behind a string of trucks carrying food and bedding, we entered smoldering Coventry. The city, with a population of nearly 130,000, was much larger than I thought it would be. We drove through water up to the hubs as broken mains sent muddy water snaking in miniature rivers down the streets. We had to detour masses of stone and brick that littered the pavement. Finally we came to a gaping hole that cut off our street. We had to park and walk.

All of us had been to Coventry before so we knew where we were. I had been in the tea shop which the mechanic's sister partly owned. If there was anything left of the shop, people there would know where she was and what had happened to her.

Damage wasn't so great just where we were walking. Ahead, however, we could see that the city had taken a terrific beating. The day was cold and a dismal dirty smoke pall hung overhead. Columns of smoke were reaching up, augmenting the pall. There were many people about, most of them in uniforms of civilian defense services. Ambulances were thick. Scores of people were wandering about, apparently looking for relations or belongings. The predominant expression on people's faces was a certain iron grimness. We sensed a glowing hatred that would burn fiercely long, long after the greatest bomb-set fire in that flame-ravaged city.

The tremendous job of restoring life to some semblance of normalcy was well under way. We passed several relief wagons where hot tea, sandwiches and cookies were being served. Heroic A.R.P. crews were everywhere, still at work, their faces gaunt and grime-covered. They hadn't stopped since the raid started.

We arrived at the tea shop, and in front of it saw an automobile that actually had been blown in two. A frail young man, the same one who had served us before, was sweeping glass into the gutter. The whole front of the quaint little shop had been blown out.

"Hello," I said. "They got your place, too."

"How d'you do, sir," he looked up, recognizing me. We had had quite a talk before. He had tried to get into the R.A.F. but was disqualified physically. "We're open for business. Come on in and have a spot of tea."

Hardly believing that this disheveled place could be open, we went inside. An elderly woman was boarding up the yawning front windows. She nodded as we took our seats at a table. The young man pointed to us and held up three fingers. She brought us three cups and poured our tea.

The young man stood beside us, resting on his broom.

"The dirty Huns gave us a hell of a bombing," he growled. "Tried to wipe us out, they did. But we can take a lot more of that."

"Looks as if you lost pretty heavily," Jim commented looking around at the fire-scarred walls.

"Knocked everything we had off the shelves," the youth said. "We put the stock back and put out the fire before it did much damage. Don't know what I'll do, though, when these clothes get dusty. Our house is burned up and everything in it. We're kind of lucky at that, you know. When you look around and see how the others got it."

"We came down here," Phil said, "looking for Miss Walmsley. Her brother at our station hasn't heard from her and he's pretty anxious."

"Haven't seen her since yesterday. She said she was going out of town. Might try her house, if you like."

He gave us the address. Finishing the tea, we paid him and left.

In a few minutes we reached the address to find the apartment house a pile of rubble. A rescue crew huddled at the base of the shattered brick building was digging frantically with shovels into the mass of stone and dirt. As we approached we heard a muffled moan. It came from somewhere inside the pile of rubble.

The digging stopped and a little cockney fellow, his face too begrimed to tell what he looked like, dropped his shovel and crawled through a hole just big enough to permit a man's body. Four men crouched at the hole's mouth, one shining a flashlight into it. They were ready to start digging immediately if a sudden cave-in trapped their comrade.

The moaning continued. It was the voice of a

woman. She sounded as if something were pressing against her, because the moan came in a gush and there were several seconds between the gasps.

We picked our way across the brick-littered street, jumped over the stream of water that gushed down the curb and around the debris.

"She badly hurt?" Phil asked a gray-haired, grim-faced workman.

" 'Fraid she is, sir," the man nodded gravely. "Been buried in there more than twelve hours. Every time we gets a hole dug to her there's a cave-in and we got to start all over. There's a beam crushing her spine. I think Herbert'll make it to her this time."

"Who is she?" Phil asked.

"Don't know yet."

"Have you taken anyone else out of there?"

"Yep, we got three elderly gentlemen and a couple of kids."

"We're looking for a Miss Walmsley who lived here," Phil said, and explained our mission.

"That's kind of bad," the workman said. "Better wait around a bit."

A stretcher was brought to the hole's entrance by a business-like looking woman in khaki. She sat down on the chest of a fallen gargoyle and began lifting first aid equipment from a box.

From somewhere inside the hole, which wasn't

more than eighteen inches across, came a muffled, " 'Ere she is. Bring a crowbar, quick."

The gray-haired man grabbed a steel bar, took a couple of deep breaths and crawled into the hole. He seemed to fill it. I saw the soles of his heavy shoes disappear in the blackness. The mass of masonry and splintered wood timbers looked as if they would collapse over the hole any instant.

After a long silence, another of the rescue crew picked his way over broken brick to the street, pulled a tin cup from his belt and proceeded to rinse his mouth with a cupful of gutter water. He gargled it with a grimace, but didn't drink any.

"Been here all night?" Jim asked when the man returned.

"Been on the job since midnight," he nodded. "We can't let people die in the ruins, you know."

Jim nodded toward a tea shop and hurried off, returning with a pot of tea and a cup. One by one the crew left their vigil and drank deeply of the hot liquid.

After several minutes a head appeared in the hole. It was proceeding toward us in jerks. Then a little fellow crawled out to where we could pull him the rest of the way. Around his shoulders was a rope, with which he was hauling something. We pulled it gently and dragged out a slight, little woman, whose eyes were shut and whose dust-covered face was drawn in agony.

The little guy looked at the uniformed woman and whispered so the other woman couldn't hear, "Maybe 'er back is broke." The uniformed woman took the victim's pulse with one hand, carefully feeling along near the spine with the other. The injured woman's eyes fluttered open. They stared wide and moved around expressionlessly, as if they saw nothing. She began whimpering just a little, like a small child.

The little cockney stood with rumpled hair, his eyes blazing down at her.

"She never 'armed no one," he grated through clenched teeth. "It don't do the bloody 'uns no good to 'arm the likes of 'er. She were a kindly sort. 'Er 'usband was killed at the last war, an' 'ere she is. I wish to 'ell I cud blarst every one of those dirty 'uns off the face of the earth. They was just born to start trouble."

"Here, have a spot of tea, Herbert," a husky worker offered soothingly. "Take it easy, Herbert."

"Tea! I don't want none o' that," Herbert cried, shaking his fist at the sky. "I wants a gat. That's what I needs. We got to blarst 'em."

"Watch yerself, Herbert," the other said. "We got

lots more work to do before dark. Maybe they'll come back tonight. We got to get things in good shape before they come again."

"Right y'are," Herbert nodded grimly. "We got our jobs to do 'ere. Where's that tea? Me throat's a bit parched."

He drank deeply. I felt disgusted with myself for what fear I had felt last night. Here this little guy, entirely oblivious of himself or the dangers of rescue work, was taking hold of himself after fourteen hours of toil and sweat because he knew there were more hours of toil and sweat ahead.

"Is this Miss Walmsley?" I asked Herbert.

He looked at me. "You a relative, sir?" he asked.

The workman we had talked to told him we were inquiring for a relative of hers.

"Miss Walmsley's in there, sir," Herbert said quietly. "She's dead."

"Are you sure it's her?" I asked.

"I'm certain. She owns the tearoom. You see, sir, I janitor 'ere at this 'ouse where she lived."

Two of the crew eased the injured woman onto a stretcher. Our offer to carry her to a hospital was refused. The crew had to report in for a new assignment. They knew where to take her.

"But there may be more people buried here," Jim said. "Shouldn't you stay and investigate?"

"There was more," said the fellow who had crawled in after Herbert. "I saw two in the cellar, both dead. We can't take time to investigate every building now. There are crews doin' that. We got to dig out quick the ones we know is alive."

We left, picking our way silently along the busy and wrecked street until we came to a crowd of some fifteen uniformed workers, digging with shovels, picks, and their hands into a huge mound of brick peculiarly suggesting an enormous grave, with a single gaunt and fire-blackened wall of four stories at the back end of it that looked like the headstone. The smell of damp, charred wood from a recent fire was heavy in the air.

On her knees and digging in broken glass with blood-smeared hands was a white-haired woman. She was whimpering to herself. I tried to help her up, telling her, "Please, madam. You can't dig that way."

She pulled away without a word and resumed scooping up glass and brick. There was blood up to her elbow where she had been cut by the glass.

"Better leave her alone, sir," one of the workmen said. "We tried to stop her. But it's no use. She's happier that way."

What we had seen and heard was beginning to get us. We hurried to a half-wrecked pub for a scotch and soda. Two A.R.P. men came in after us, ordered drinks, downed them in a gulp and hurried out, wiping their grimy faces on grimier sleeves. The Scotch bartender refused to accept pay from them.

"You know," Jim said slowly, "for sheer guts those boys can't be beat by all the armed forces in the world. They do their work in a hell of fire and explosions and can't even take time out to fight back."

"It's not human," Phil agreed. "I couldn't do it. It's a man's instinct to fight back."

"It's whut you Amuricans call teamwurk," put in the bartender through his burly mustache. "Ye ken the game of rugby. The backs, such as you gentlemen, carry the ball, the offensive. The for'ds do the durty wurk so ye kin make the goals."

We talked a little more with the Scotch bartender and left. While we had been in the pub the face of a four-story building had slid onto the street we had walked through. Strings of smoke wriggled through the mass and up into the murk-laden air. Several blocks ahead firemen were battling a ruddy blaze. We could see them outlined against the dull glow. One fellow atop a tall extension ladder was playing a hose through the remnants of a window. A few feet in front of him was a naked unsupported wall that leaned outward and looked as if it were going to fall forward and crush him.

Where we stood the street was deserted except for

a couple of urchins, a boy and girl, about six or seven years old, climbing over heaps of brick. Both were raggedly dressed and indescribably dirty. Their faces were covered with soot. Although it was cold, even through our coats, all the girl had on was a dress. The boy wore overalls and a dirty shirt. The girl pulled the ragged remnants of what must have been a doll.

"Where's your daddy?" Jim asked, putting his hand on the boy's shoulder.

"He worked yesterday. He should be back soon," the boy answered, lifting smoke-reddened eyes to us.

"And your mother, where is she?"

"She was asleep and they took her away."

"This your sister?" I asked quickly.

"Sure. I'm takin' care of her."

"We'd better take 'em along with us," Phil said. "We can't leave 'em here."

"Oh, but we gotta stay!" the boy pleaded. "When daddy comes back he won't know where to find us if we ain't here. We live here," he added with finality.

The kid pointed at a shambles of brick that probably had once been an apartment house. It evidently had burned and then collapsed.

"I'll go find somebody to help them," I said. "You fellows wait here."

I started off down the littered street, looking for

some woman who understood children better than we did. An ambulance passed me. Bundles of human beings were packed inside. There must have been eight or nine of them. The car rolled through a billow of dark smoke which hung over the street.

People were working just inside the smoke. As I approached, I saw several men with masks. They were digging. Three uniformed and weary-looking women sat on a near-by doorstep.

I told the women about the children and a stout one who introduced herself as Mrs. MacDonald came back with me. When we arrived where the children were, Phil had taken off his overcoat and wrapped it around the youngsters. When the little boy saw us he stood up, protectively holding his sister's hand.

"Mrs. MacDonald, we want you to take this money," I said as the three of us gave her all our change, "and see that these kids get cleaned up and have something to eat. I don't think they've eaten all day. You may have to bring the food here as they refuse to leave."

Mrs. MacDonald took off her tin hat. "You see," she said, squatting down by the kids, "your daddy gave me this hat to bring to you. You recognize it as his, don't you?"

"Why yes," the little boy was delighted. "That looks like his."

"Of course," nodded Mrs. MacDonald. "He wants you to be all cleaned up for him. Now you come along with me."

"But," the boy protested, "what if he comes while we ain't here?"

"Why, these kind gentlemen will stay here and tell him you're with me. It will be all right."

A little dubiously, the kids allowed themselves to be led away. They glanced back at us frequently as they walked off. We stayed until they had disappeared.

"Everybody around here works overtime," Phil remarked. "It's the same spirit the C.O. has."

We looked at each other and knew we'd be joining him as quickly as we could get back to the airdrome. That is, after we'd broken the bad news to Walmsley. Poor guy.

Chapter XII

FIRST CASUALTIES

IT WAS nearly three weeks later, in early December, when I got my next leave. Four of us went down to London. By this time the British lion, despite its badly singed mane, was roaring at the enemy across the Channel with increased defiance. The roar was actual, for the R.A.F. had grown phenomenally and was making heavy night bombing sweeps over Germany and German-occupied countries.

At a London hotel bar we had the unexpected pleasure of meeting one of the ace fighter pilots of the Royal Air Force, a man who deserves extraordinary credit for bravery and for perseverance against great odds. He was Squadron Leader Douglas R. S. Bader, D.S.O., D.F.C. When Squadron Leader Bader rose from his seat to greet us, he had to lift himself erect with the aid of his hands. He had two artificial legs!

He told us how he had been injured as an acrobatic

pilot, the injuries being so severe that both legs had to be amputated. It was several years before he could fly. He took it up again by himself, just to prove to the Royal Air Corps that he could still handle a plane. And what a pilot that fellow was!

He described how he and his squadron of Canadian Hurricane pilots ran smack into the only bomber formation the Italians sent up for a daylight assault over England.

"The Benitos, you know," Squadron Leader Bader told us, "wanted to help their Nazi ally take care of London and the R.A.F. The Germans knew the antique Italian Marchetti bombers wouldn't have a show against our Hurricanes or Spitfires, but they gave their assent to the undertaking. They told their comrades-in-arms that they would have to map their own strategy and send their own fighter escort, if they thought they needed one.

"We were on patrol, a full squadron of us, and ran into eighteen Marchettis over the Channel. Somehow we let three of them get away. We didn't lose a single fighter."

That meant fifteen out of eighteen downed! In every aerial encounter of this war where modern, heavily-armed and fast aircraft have fought older, flimsier planes the results have been devastating.

Later, inspecting some of the London air raid shelters, we found them vastly improved in sanitation, safety and comforts. There were more of them, and people no longer were packed in like bullets in a machine-gun belt. The raids were lighter and less frequent, enabling Londoners to catch up on the sleep they had lost during the heavy September bombings. The great city was much more cheerful.

We returned to our airdrome just in time to hear a talk by an American-born visitor, Lady Astor, who told us that although the United States might not realize it, this was the greatest hour of trial for the English-speaking race, America's turn would come next. Prophetic words, these, spoken almost a year to the day before the attack on Pearl Harbor!

The Eagle Squadron was growing. Among the American fellows joining up were Samuel Alfred Maureillo, Astoria, Long Island; Peter Provenzano, a Chicago stunt pilot; Nathaniel Maranz, New York City, and two more Californians, William Nichols of San Carlos, and Victor Robert Bono of San Francisco.

We were making some practice flights and a few patrols, but in general the weather was keeping the Germans at home, so there wasn't much flying to be done. There was none at all on Christmas, neither the British nor Germans sending even one aircraft across the Channel. There was a big Christmas dinner at our airdrome and in the evening a dance.

The first week in January Phil Leckrone, Bud Orbison, and I hopped off on a semi-cloudy day to make some mock attacks—and some real ones if we spotted any Jerries.

I was acting as section leader and led the vic up to 20,000 feet, where I ordered an echelon starboard formation. In this battle formation the aircraft were flying single file, but stepped off to the right. Although camouflaging prevented our seeing it from this altitude, the airdrome was almost directly below.

I peeled off to port for a make-believe beam attack, coming out of the dive and rolling over, keeping the aircraft's nose on a cloud tuft near the horizon. That was the target. Bud and Phil were close behind. My Hurricane dropped away in a dive and I blacked out cold. Regaining consciousness, I found my body slumped low in the seat. My head was paining severely from the quick drop of 7,000 feet.

Putting the Hurricane in a steep climb I came up to 20,000 and leveled off, waiting for the other two fellows to reform behind me. While cruising in a wide circle I gazed over the great expanse of bright sky scenery, spotted with clouds far below. Couldn't see a Jerry anywhere.

Bud's Hurricane slid up behind my starboard wing. Through the rear vision mirror I could see it bobbing along in perfect position. He was number three man so he left a space between us for Phil. Phil should have been in place before Bud, but Phil's breakaway might have been faster, which could have kept him blacked out longer.

Tilting the Hurricane a little so I could look down, I saw Phil's aircraft zooming up behind us. Swell. For a moment I thought something might have happened to him. I watched through the mirror as he climbed a little above Bud to come over him into position. His wings were wobbling a little. He'd probably lost too much speed in his climb and no doubt he was gunning the motor to bring her out of it.

As it approached Bud's tail, Phil's aircraft lost several feet altitude. I glanced over my shoulder anxiously. He was much too close to Bud. What the devil was he trying to do? Phil's Hurricane was a bare two feet above Bud's greenhouse as he edged forward.

"Phil!" I yelled into the mike. "Pull up! You're almost hitting Bud!"

Phil's plane moved ahead and almost had passed Bud when it's tail dropped sharply, striking Bud's port wing! Horrified, I saw Bud's aileron ripped off, and at the same time the entire tail assembly of Phil's plane broke off.

Phil's Hurricane immediately went into a flat spin, its motor pulling the aircraft in a small circle as it spun down. Although Bud almost had lost control of his aircraft, he managed to right it by using only the starboard aileron. He raised his damaged port wing and started to descend.

"Jack!" Bud's voice came over the R.T. "Phil's in trouble."

I could see plainly that both of them were in a bad way. But Bud was managing to hold his own, so I went into a steep dive after Phil. There he was below, his tail-less aircraft continuing its flat spin. Why didn't Phil slide the hatch and bail out? I could see him in the greenhouse, slumped forward over his stick as though he were unconscious.

I came out of the dive and circled outside his aircraft. He hit a cloud and spun on through it. I went through the cloud in a hurry, not wanting to tangle with that wrecked Hurricane.

"Phil! Phil!" I called. "Bail out! Jump! You're in danger!"

I kept calling his name and yelling "danger," trying to bring him out of it. Down, down spun the damaged aircraft. I followed, keeping as close to it as

[203]

possible. The altimeter read 2,000 feet! I yelled and pleaded some more. His aircraft was descending comparatively slowly, its wings and fuselage horizontal, the propeller uselessly flailing the air.

A few hundred feet from the ground I knew what was going to happen. It was too late now for him to bail out. I called operations to send an ambulance and crash wagon. Apparently Bud had landed safely and had notified the field of what was happening. An ambulance and wagon were on the way.

Relentlessly down toward a wide field not far from the airdrome Phil's plane spun. There was its shadow on the tall, dry grass, closing in toward it as it descended. Then it smacked the ground, bounced in a cloud of dust and grass, and broke apart. There was no fire. I continued circling to guide the ambulance and truck until I saw them speed across the field to the wreckage.

I climbed to 2,000 feet, made a dive over the spot, pulled up, and did a roll, a final salute to the first casualty of the Eagle Squadron. Then I headed for the airdrome.

The investigation into the cause of the fatal crash, as far as I could learn, was inconclusive because the Hurricane had been so badly wrecked. The most probable explanation was that something had happened to Phil's oxygen equipment. Perhaps his tube had become kinked, cutting off his supply. That could have caused him to faint in the high altitude and crash into Bud.

The funeral was held on a cold January day and the procession which left the airdrome for the small church at a near-by town was a long one. First was a military truck carrying the coffin, which was draped with an American and a British flag. Our entire squadron marched behind the truck. Back of us were members of the station's other two squadrons. Next came 200 Waafs, many aircraftsmen, and lastly the eight men in Phil's ground crew.

After brief services in the church, the coffin was taken to an open grave near by. We marched by and saluted. Soldiers fired a volley and taps was played as Phil was lowered into the ground he was willing to give his life to save. A fine fellow and a grand flyer.

A few mornings later a group of us were in the hut. A section from the British Spitfire squadron had taken off a few minutes before on dawn patrol.

"Squadron ———! Red Section! Scramble!" came sharply over the Tannoy loud-speaker. It was the first battle call for the Eagle Squadron! All our previous assignments had been patrols. Luke, Flight Lieutenant B., a Britisher with twelve victories to his credit, and I formed the Red Section.

The three of us ran out in our heavy flying gear, clamping on helmets. Our aircraft were on the line and I grabbed the parachute off the wing and began strapping it on hurriedly, my flight sergeant helping me. I swung into the "office." B. was roaring his Hurricane out and down the runway.

I pushed the throttle and followed him, saluting my crew, who were all out there watching the take-off. Luke was rolling along beside me. I was in number two position at the right of B. and Luke was number three. I set the propeller at full fine and the carburetor boost and r.p.m.'s at 2,400.

The three of us took off together in a vic. Here was the flight I had worked months for! The first real crack at the enemy. Perhaps it would give us a chance to even up the score for Phil.

Up we zoomed in a wide circle, still in a tight vic. My eyes were on B.'s starboard wing. I heard him inform operations we were air-borne. Operations vectored us southeast. That meant we were going over the Channel. I felt my right hand grow tense as the fingers gripped the control stick. With my left I was jockeying the throttle to keep in tight formation behind B.

We roared up to 18,000 feet. I had the oxygen on and was pulling in deep breaths, wanting all my wits about me. Far below I could see the ragged coastline of Britain. Here and there was a light, flat patch of ground, near the coast. These were the old airdromes that had been abandoned during the heavy German blitz. Along their edges were concrete posts and stretched across them at different elevations were heavy cables. If a Jerry attempted to land on any of them, his aircraft would be torn to shreds and completely wrecked.

We were thundering along at better than 300 miles an hour when I heard a crackling in the earphones. Then came an excited "Tallyho!" I recognized the voice. Yes, it was "Cocky," who had led the Spitfire patrol up from our airdrome. He was attacking the enemy! My heart sank. I fervently hoped there would be something left to attack when we got there. I could hear the scream of his motor over the radio, then a dull rumble that must have been his machine-guns firing.

We got another vector which changed our course northward two degrees. I couldn't take my eyes off B.'s wing long enough to scan the sky for the combat.

"Red Two and Three! Red One calling. Line astern!"

It was B.'s voice. He was ordering us into a battle formation. I slid to the rear of his aircraft. Through the rear vision mirror I saw Luke slide back of me.

"Medal Control! Medal Control! White Leader calling. Dornier 17 down."

It was "Cocky" informing operations he had downed the Jerry bomber. I looked below and saw a long black line in the blue water. It was the convoy. But I couldn't see any other aircraft except ours.

"Hello, Red Leader. Medal Control calling. Patrol Huntley. Is that understood?"

Huntley was the code name for the convoy. In line astern we began circling the convoy of some forty vessels. A few miles distant was the Dutch coast. The R.A.F. had such complete mastery of the air that it was safe to bring this big line of ships down the east coast.

Very softly through the R.T., I could hear B. cursing for getting to the scene too late. I felt very much let down, myself.

I spotted an aircraft climbing toward us, its wings just a razor line against the sea. B. changed our course so he could dive on it in an instant if it proved to be a Nazi fighter. From its small graceful size and dihedral or up-tilt of the wings I identified it as a Spitfire. It climbed up to our altitude, impudently wiggled its wings and sped off westward.

The R.T. crackled as it came to life and a British voice announced, "Better get here sooner next time, Hurricane pilots." The Spitfire pilot was rubbing it in a little too much.

B. ordered us into loose search formation so each aircraft could be farther from the other two, giving each pilot a chance to look for Jerries. For nearly an hour we made a wide circle over the crawling convoy until we were relieved by another Eagle Squadron section composed of Gus Daymond, Andy Mamedoff, and Stan Kolendorski.

Instead of heading straight home when the others arrived, B. dove sharply seaward. Wondering what was up, Luke and I followed. We were slanting down at nearly 400 miles an hour when B. pulled gradually out, a few hundred feet above the sea. Then I saw what he was after. It was an empty boat about sixteen feet long, lolling on the water. We had orders to destroy anything on the sea that might be a menace to shipping.

"Red Two. Red One calling. Destroy that boat. Perhaps that will ease your disappointment a bit. If your marksmanship isn't good, Red Three will finish the job."

I banked and came around to get a bead on the target. I unsnapped the safety on the firing button and moved the ring from safe to fire position. Then I turned on the gunsights. Squinting through the sights, I dipped when 150 yards from the bobbing boat. With my thumb I pressed the firing button. Immediately the aircraft vibrated slightly as the Brownings went into action. In a split second the boat literally disappeared, blasted to bits by the concentrated fire.

I climbed up and rejoined the formation and we headed west for the home airdrome. In addition to the roar of my motor I could hear the scream of wind through the eight gun ports. Blowing an empty boat to pieces had not eased the disappointment at missing the real show. I began to feel that I was making a habit of getting on the scene too late or muffing it when I did arrive in time. But I was still alive and someone had said comfortingly that while there's life there's hope.

The rest of January passed quietly enough. Except for additional men joining up and a few routine patrols, nothing much happened.

It was a foggy day in early February that Bud Orbison and D. went up with one of the new members of the squadron. When they came back, D. and Bud circled the airdrome while the new boy came in for a precarious landing in the mist. Just as the fledgling came in, Bud's Hurricane spun out of the fog and crashed on the edge of the airdrome. When we reached the aircraft, we found Bud dead. This was a tough blow to me as Bud and I were particularly good friends. Apparently his plane had lost too much flying speed as he anxiously tried to observe the landing of the new pilot.

There was another funeral at the little church in the near-by town and a new grave in the cemetery set aside for Eagle Squadron pilots.

Chapter XIII

TALLYHO

AFTER a week of being confined to the ground by bad weather, we were awakened one night by the blasts of high-explosive bombs and the "whap! whap!" percussion of antiaircraft fire. Our brick officers' quarters rocked and shook with the crescendo. This meant that the storms which had grounded the Nazis were breaking, that Jerry probably would be back during the daylight hours to make up for lost time, and that we would see action after a week of restless waiting.

The thunderous pounding stopped shortly after midnight and we snatched a bit of sleep.

An hour before dawn the batman brought in the cup of tea, now our "official" getting up drink. Luke climbed out of bed and we began the cumbersome ritual of getting into our flying togs.

I stuck my head out the window and discovered it wasn't cold enough for the fur-lined Irving suit.

We dressed in thick silk teddy bears and fireproof sidkas. Pulling on our boots, into which we stuffed maps, and carrying helmets, Mae Wests and gloves and mittens, we headed downstairs for breakfast. We found most of the boys unusually voluble, keyed up at the prospect of action.

Breakfast done we hurried out into the approaching dawn to check the aircraft and to see if the bombing had harmed the airdrome. It hadn't, although my sergeant pilot informed me that a near-by dummy airfield, on which were four dummy planes made of old wooden boxes, had been blasted to bits.

As I crawled into the Hurricane's cockpit, my mechanic sang out his customary, "She's hot and ready, sir." Since Jerry was afraid to send over bomber formations during the day, I set the gunsights for thirty-two and one-half feet, the wing span of an Me. 109. We were more apt to run into them than any other type of Nazi aircraft.

Laying the parachute on the wing where it could be grabbed quickly, I hurried—you do everything in a hurry over here excepting the waiting—to the airdrome office and signed the "700 sheet," first making sure that every member of my ground crew had his name down. Luke and Flight Lieutenant B., the other two pilots of Red Section, signed up. B., as section leader, telephoned operations, "Red Section now in readiness."

We went into the dispersal hut; nothing to do but wait expectantly. For awhile the favorite between-flight diversion was teaching the British pilots how to shoot dice. They were too lucky so we dropped this game for dominoes or cards.

About two hours passed. Suddenly the long-expected metallic voice—the one we'd waited a week to hear—snapped over the Tannoy loud-speaker:

"Squadron ———, Red Section. Scramble!"

That was us! I caught Luke's triumphant grin as he jumped up. He and I ran out to our aircraft, pulling on helmets and gloves. I grabbed my 'chute and climbed into its harness. My big Merlin Rolls Royce motor already was ticking beautifully.

I got aboard and adjusted the Sutton harness, fastening it loosely so I could lean forward to fight off blackouts. I revved up the motor, holding the brakes on. Attaching the oxygen tube to the tank and plugging the radio cord to the R.T. set, I eased off the brakes.

Like a long-caged bird anxious for the sky's freedom, the big Hurricane rolled down the runway, gathering speed with each revolution of the propeller. Flipping the magneto switches to test them, I adjusted the propeller at full fine and set the carburetor boost. The motor was only about two-thirds open on the take-off. B. was ahead and Luke beside me. In a vic we hopped off, boosting the planes into a steep climb. Luke and I were concentrating so intensely on B.'s wing tips that he could have flown us into a mountain and we'd never have seen it.

B. called operations by its code name of the day, Battle Control, and reported we were air-borne.

Later operations asked, "Hello, Red Leader. Battle Control calling. Are you receiving me?"

"Hello, Battle Control, Red Leader answering. Receiving you loud and clear. Over."

"Hello, Red Leader. Vector 110. Is that understood?"

"Hello, Battle Control, Red Leader answering. Understand vector 110. Listening out."

Now we knew where we were going. We'd been circling for altitude until we got the vector. I set the compass at 110, which would bring us over the North Sea. We knew we'd been assigned to one of two jobs, either to patrol or to get a bomber that was preying on a convoy. These are the usual North Sea assignments.

At 9,000 feet a cloud bank swallowed us. It took us two minutes to reach it. Luke and I were flying

very tight, our wing tips three feet back of and inside
B.'s ailerons. You've got to fly this way in the soup
or you'll lose one another. And a lone Hurricane is
just a piece of cake for Jerry. In the last war, air
battles consisted of spectacular two-plane dogfights.
Today these are the exception. Most modern fighting
is done in teams, and the R.A.F. has developed formation flying and combat teamwork to the highest de-
gree of efficiency the world has ever known.

I felt a bumping and scraping. It was my wing tip
touching B.'s wing. The thought of a crumpled wing
was most unpleasant. Three times I'd found paint
from his wing on mine. I moved back into position
and turned the oxygen on.

At 14,000 feet we burst through the clouds into
the bright world of the upper air, a world with fan-
tastic cloud landscapes of cottony valleys and billowy
mountains. The scene dazzled me. This was the battleground of the second World War. At 20,000 feet
we leveled off. I was a little lightheaded from the
quick climb, although I had kept the oxygen intake
at 5,000 feet ahead of the actual altitude. A dial shows
the amount of oxygen you are taking in. The higher
the altitude, the more oxygen you turn on.

No enemy aircraft were visible, but B. ordered the
section into line astern. You never could tell when

Jerry would come swarming out of the clouds. Luke and I swung our Hurricanes in a line behind B., Luke being in the "rear man Charley" spot, protecting our tails. Then the radio crackled:

"Hello, Red Leader. Battle Control calling. Are you receiving me?"

B. reported he was.

"Hello, Red Leader. Angels one zero. Bandit."

An enemy aircraft at 10,000 feet! It must be a prowler over the North Sea. Down we shot into the clouds again. I boosted the throttle and the Hurricane jumped ahead, keeping close behind B. I turned the safety catch on the firing button, snapped on the gunsight and looked over the instruments quickly, my subconscious mind doing most of the work. The motor was heating a bit, but there was no time to do anything about it. Since I had my gunsight adjusted for the wing span of an Me. 109, I knew I would have to reset it before making an attack. Apparently there was only one bandit, and it must be a bomber whose wing span might be double that of a Messerschmitt fighter.

We came under the clouds at 11,000 feet and leveled off. Better stay near the stratus until we sized up the situation. Below was a great slab of sea, with a ragged, dark coastline to the west. England. About

twelve miles offshore were black streaks which resembled a stream of ants. They were ships in a convoy.

There! About five miles ahead and 3,000 feet below
scooted a black bug. I squinted to make out what it
was. It looked like a Dornier 17 heavy bomber, one
of the nastiest aircraft to tackle. Manned by four or
five men, it was heavily gunned and armored. I
glanced up. There might be an escort of Messerschmitts just inside that sullen cloud curtain. No time
for reconnoitering. We slanted toward the bomber—
yes, it was a Dornier. We didn't want him to see us
until we got closer. If only he took his time getting
the range of the convoy, we could swoop down and
nail him before he did any damage. I hoped none of
the Spitfire boys were around to try and spoil our
chase.

Suddenly the bomber dropped his nose in a steep
dive toward the convoy. He must have spotted us and
he wanted to get a vessel or two before going home.
I saw the black cross on top of his starboard wing as
he went into the plunge. His two big propellers
glinted menacingly for a moment, like a wolf baring
his teeth.

B. yelled, "Tallyho!" and dove after him. I followed pulling the teat, the auxiliary throttle that cut
loose all 1,250 horsepower. We vaulted downstairs,

our Merlins screaming. Just then the unhurried voice
of operations reported over the radio: "Hello, Red
Leader. Battle Control calling. You should be in
vicinity of Tunbridge Wells and bandit." Tunbridge
Wells, a small English town, was the code name for
this convoy.

B. called, "Hello, Battle Control. Red Leader answering. We're chasing bandit!" Operations dropped
his formal answer, merely saying, "Good luck."

It was a race now to see who got to the convoy
first. The Dornier was away below us and was hard
to see, being painted blue-gray, the color of the sea.
The Germans had a tricky habit of camouflaging their
planes for every special job. We were gaining fast.
Suddenly my Hurricane rocked violently. It steadied
and started rocking again. I spotted a puff of smoke
from a vessel in the convoy. He was shooting at the
bomber, but his antiaircraft shells were bursting
somewhere near us.

The firing stopped as the Dornier and we approached the long line of ships. The Dornier cut
loose a whole stick of four bombs. He wasn't wasting his time aiming and I knew the bombs would fall
wide. We were about three-quarters of a mile from
him now. B. veered off from the direct chase, diving
for the first freighters in the convoy, trying to cut

the Dornier off from his prey. Seeing that we were too close, the Jerry banked away toward home, dropping his other bomb stick and an aerial torpedo to lighten his load. The bombs sent up harmless geysers of water a mile from the nearest freighter. The torpedo, I knew, broke when it hit the water after being dropped from 2,000 feet. We had won the first round. Now to get the Dornier. We banked after him.

He had dropped so close to the sea that it looked as if he would ram into it. He leveled off a scant twenty feet above the choppy waves, his starboard wing tip almost cutting the water as he turned directly toward his base. These Dorniers could move fast. Quickly I set the gunsight for a fifty-nine-foot wing span.

Close to the water the Dornier was a tough target. We couldn't dive on him or we would ram into the sea. The only attack to make was directly astern, trying to pick off the top turret gunner before he blasted us. Then we could get at the pilot.

We were closing in fast. He was less than a mile away. B. began leveling off and I hauled back a little on the stick, to stay astern of him. It was hard to pull against the 400-plus-mile-an-hour wind velocity. I could see the Dornier's gunner now in his plastic glass blister, his hands on his twin cannon triggers.

As we came gradually out of the dive, centrifugal force dragged on my body. My hands grew heavy and my jaw sagged. Mustn't black out! I took a deep breath and yelled—anything to build up blood pressure so the blood wouldn't leave my brain. Another danger presented itself. We were much too close to the water. If we ever hit the propeller back-wash of the bomber, it would bounce us into the sea.

The German opened fire, smoke from his tracers looping up at B., who threw his Hurricane into a criss-cross to throw off the Jerry's aim. B. started firing; his tracer bullets showed he was firing into the blister. Then B. was past the gunner and it was my turn.

I moved the stick right, then left, and alternated foot pressure on the rudder to keep the gunner in the sights. I could even see his tense face. His lips were parted, his teeth clenched as he sawed his fire-spouting cannons back and forth. I pressed the firing button with my thumb, hurling explosives, ball, incendiary, armor-piercing, and tracer bullets at him. The noise was like muffled high-pitched drums and the plane vibrated and slowed from the recoil. The tracers' chemical smoke trails showed the fire sweeping under the Dornier.

Abandoning caution to get a more accurate aim, I

stopped the criss-cross and nosed the Hurricane right at him. He was only about 100 yards away now. There was a loud pow! And a splintering sound, like hailstones on a drum. He must have hit me. But I couldn't see where. My bullets were streaming into his blister, tearing great rents in the plastic glass.

Just as I swept over him, he fell back, arms upraised. I slipped up and to the side. A black curtain dropped over my eyes as I came around, almost in a vertical bank. I eased the stick forward to come to, knowing that Luke was giving the pilot the works.

I glanced back to see Luke almost cutting off the Dornier's tail with his prop, he was flying so close to him. The bomber was still flying. We didn't get him on the first attack.

As I followed B. down for another attack I heard Luke yell over the radio, "Red Leader. Red Three calling. Bandits over the French Coast!" I looked to the east. Nine planes in three vics were coming toward us, one vic far in advance of the others. The Dornier must have radioed for help. The planes still were several miles away but it wouldn't take a minute for them to get here. We had to work fast.

B.'s Hurricane thundered down on the Dornier's tail. I saw two Germans dragging the gunner's body from his seat. They were going to replace him. If they succeeded in doing this before we got the pilot, the Dornier was as good as safe on its home airdrome. The pilot would be protected by the new rear gunner until the Jerry fighter planes arrived. B. dove low over the Dornier's tail and gave the pilot's cockpit a long burst, sliding up and to the side again. Before I could start firing, the Dornier's wings wiggled slightly, the nose dropped slowly. He smacked the water, sheets of spray exploding up from his fuselage. He bounced twice and settled on the choppy sea. B. got him that time. Soon he would sink.

Heading upstairs in a hurry after B., I spotted the first Jerry section of three aircraft slanting down to attack us. These aircraft were smaller than an Me. 109 and they were painted white. I had never seen them before. They must be the new, faster Heinkel 113 fighters we'd heard about.

I closed in behind B. and Luke was right on my tail. We were low on petrol and bullets and we had finished our job, so the better part of valor was to head for home quickly. Besides our planes had been damaged and might not be able to stand the terrific strain of combat. Below us the remainder of the Dornier crew launched a rubber life boat.

B. leveled off to gain speed and pointed for home. I followed, nearly deafened by the scream of air through the cowling where the cannon shell had penetrated, and by the shriek from the machine-gun mouths where the patches had been shot away.

The Jerries kept coming, so B. banked quickly and started circling. Now Jerry couldn't get on our tail because each one of us was protecting the other's tail. The three Heinkels veered away. They didn't like our circle.

"Red Two and Three, Red One calling. Maintain tight formation, line astern!"

As one Heinkel got a little below us, B. suddenly straightened out and dove for it. Luke and I were right behind him. B. got in a long burst. The two other Heinkels immediately dove for B. I picked one Jerry and Luke the other. I got in one quick burst of fire on my Heinkel's tail. Then it power-dived out of range. In fact all three Heinkels veered off and hurried away. We quickly reformed behind B. Apparently they weren't too anxious to tangle.

B. called Battle Control, got the response and announced, "Hello, Battle Control. Red Leader calling. Dornier 17 down. See pilots in rubber boat. Bandits in vicinity." Operations might send a launch or flying boat after them.

Luke and I both reported that our petrol was running low. Luke added that his port wing had been

[224]

badly ripped. I hoped everything would hold together until we landed.

We left the sea and the Jerries, vowing to be back for them later, and started flying over England. Operations was vectoring us home. Although the countryside was honeycombed with airdromes, we couldn't spot one from up here. Clever artists had blended buildings, airdromes, and gun emplacements with paint and secret camouflaging materials to look like a checkerboard of innocent farm plots, separated by hedges. Operations informed us we were above our airdrome and we circled down over what looked like a pasture, with hedges and haystacks. At 800 feet we made out the runway. Circling the field, we lowered our landing gear and flaps and came in at 100 miles an hour for a power landing. We slid across the field and my wheels rumbled pleasantly on the runway as the plane settled down. We were back! The clock showed we'd been gone only forty minutes!

We taxied to our camouflaged, sandbagged hangars, where the ground crews greeted us with cheers. They had heard the shriek of wind through the gun ports. I felt let down and tired from nervous exhaustion. My hands were clammy and the helmet seemed very heavy and tight. There was much conversation as we climbed out and inspected the damage. The crews swarmed over the aircraft and found that all three planes bore marks of the fight. The shell that had burst in my ship struck just ahead of the hatch and not six inches from where my forehead had been pressed against the gunsight rest. A close call. The floor was filled with glass fragments. Luke and I were assigned new planes until ours were repaired.

After checking the new aircraft, we made out combat reports and notified operations that we were in readiness again. Then we returned to the dispersal hut to wait for something else to happen.

Chapter XIV

SHORTY LOVES A SCRAMBLE

"HELLO, White Leader. Camel Control calling. Can't land at 'dump' because of fog. Vector two, one, zero, fifteen miles to emergency airdrome." The R.A.F. controller's face was grave as he finished talking and listened to his earphones. He looked up and shook his head. "Shorty and his boys are out of petrol and must land here." He turned to a telephone. "Order the crash wagon to stand by."

Jim McGinnis and I rushed from the operations room into the cold February fog outside. We half felt our way to the airdrome's apron to join a score of pilots and maintenance personnel who were trying to squint up through the mist.

Overhead I heard the whining roar of three Hurricane motors. In two of the aircraft were student pilots of the Eagle Squadron. In the third was Section Leader "Shorty" Vernon Keough. Visibility had been good when the three took off more than an hour before. The students had been practicing beam attacks under the critical eye of Shorty. But great curtains of mist had descended over the airdrome. Soon they would merge into a gray mass. They already had overhead.

As the crash wagon's starter whined and the motor burst into life, out of the east came a dark blob that resolved itself into the murky silhouette of an aircraft. It skimmed low for a landing, coming in much too fast. It struck the runway, leaned hard to port and bounced into the air. There was a defiant roar as the student pilot gunned his Merlin, taking off again into the mist.

We followed the Hurricane around the airdrome by the noise of its motor. There were duller drones of the other two aircraft higher up, and also the ominous purr of the crash wagon.

I stared to the east. Here came the aircraft again. This time not so fast. A mist curtain obscured it a moment. There it was, streaking along the runway, heaving a little as if loath to stay on the ground. But she was down safely.

Now the operator by radio would notify Shorty that the first student had landed. He already must have done so, for a second blob almost immediately stained the gray blanket to the east.

"They must be awfully low on petrol to come in so close together," Jim cried excitedly.

The second ship thundered in at better than 100 miles an hour, the pilot trying to make the landing ten feet in the air. Mist swallowed him as he was forced to gun his motor and try again.

It was agony to watch. Shorty, of course, like a ship's captain would be the last to seek safety. His tanks probably were drier than those of his students because he was doing the demonstrating.

Here came the second student again. The fog had thickened so we caught only an occasional indistinct shadow of the plane. For a second I saw it racing along the runway, much too fast. Unconsciously, we listened for a crash. There was none. The fog closed in just as we heard a swishing sound, as if an aircraft's tail were skidding on the runway.

The mist was so thick now we relied solely on sound to learn what was happening. Suddenly there was silence, except for the crash wagon's motor. Then came two quick pops from above us, followed by the rev-up of a motor that was starving for petrol, then three quick backfires.

"His engine's conking!" someone shouted.

A sudden gust whipped the fog off the landing strip and Jim and I squatted down, peering along the ground. Jim grabbed my arm and pointed west. On

[229]

the runway, its landing gear flattened, sat a Hurricane. Its pilot, apparently unhurt, was running for the safety of the apron. It was the second student's aircraft. Involuntarily Jim started up and I grabbed him. There was nothing we could do. The Hurricane on the runway was right in Shorty's path. That is, if he could make a dead-stick landing, an almost impossible feat in a Hurricane, even on a clear day.

"Why didn't he use his 'chute when he had a chance?" Jim demanded, knowing as well as I that if there was any chance of saving a plane, Shorty would take that chance.

"He'll make it safe, boys!" shouted Andy Mamedoff. "Remember what his mother used to say when he got lost jumping from his parachute."

We all remembered. Shorty frequently told us how, when he was a parachute jumper in America a wayward wind would carry him and his 'chute into some remote spot and no one would hear from him for a couple of days. People who came to comfort his mother in Brooklyn were in turn consoled by her calm words, "He'll come back. He always does." And he always did. But his present predicament was more dangerous than a 'chute-landing in a farmer's back yard.

Out of the corner of my right eye I saw a shadow—

the wheels of a plane. That was all I could see in the murk. The wheels, traveling at high speed, appeared to be hanging from the fog, like a blind man's finger groping for the earth. They reached down, touched the runway. I heard the clonk of shock absorbers. At almost the same instant the tail wheel descended. Fog blurred the wheels a moment. Another gust ripped the mist aside, revealing the aircraft speeding along the runway toward the damaged Hurricane.

"Now he'll see the plane and get out of the way!" some fellow yelled.

"No he won't," I shouted. "He can't see over the nose of his aircraft when she's in landing position!"

Like an arrow streaking for its target, Shorty's aircraft rolled for the Hurricane. He smacked it at about seventy miles an hour and plowed half through it, tossing bits of metal fabric and strutting high in the air.

We all tore across the field, following the crash wagon. There might be a fire and we must get Shorty out—if he was still alive.

Jim and I reached the wreck and helped rip off the telescoped hatch. Shorty was slumped forward in his cockpit. Jim pulled him back and someone unsnapped the seat strap. As we lifted him out, Shorty opened his eyes and grinned a little.

"Never a dull moment, boys," he said. That was Shorty for you!

"Not when you're around," I growled with relieved gruffness. "You damn near broke your neck."

"My gad, 'e's a wee mite of a feller!" blurted one of the new mechanics who had just arrived at the station. He said it in a low voice but Shorty overheard him.

On his feet now and shaking off the hands that tried to steady him, Shorty turned haughtily to the mechanic, drawing himself up to his full four feet, eleven inches.

"You may be taller than me down here. But up there"—he looked up—"we're all the same size."

That night the near tragedy was forgotten as Shorty was feted as the "unofficial mascot" of the Handley Page Hampden bomber boys at their officers' mess.

"Shorty Keough now will give us a song!" a bomber pilot sang out. Three of them hoisted Shorty to the top of a piano. Someone handed him a drink and a dozen airmen burst into "Roll Out the Barrel." Shorty just sat on the piano, sipping his drink. At the song's end there was a rousing cheer for him, which he acknowledged by nodding his head and raising his glass.

Andy Mamedoff and Gene Tobin, the Eagle pilots who saw brief service in France with Shorty as members of the French Armée de l'Air, laughed.

"Shorty doesn't mind being treated as the mascot here," recalled Andy. "But remember when we first signed up with the R.A.F. and the British enlistment officer took one look at him and said, 'Who's this, a mascot?' Old Shorty snorted, 'Mascot, hell. I'm a flyer!'"

Next morning Shorty, Andy and I, as Red Section, were ordered aloft. Revving his short legs up to twice the speed of ours, Shorty kept up with us as we ran out of the dispersal hut to our aircraft. I winked at Andy as Shorty carefully inspected his cockpit seat to see that his two pillows were in place. Without them and his parachute to sit on, he would be too low in his seat to see out.

Shorty hopped in and roared his aircraft down the runway. He was our section leader and we pulled in behind him. Up we went, Shorty lifting his ship into a steep spiral climb. I heard him tell operations we were air-borne and a few seconds later we got a vector to head southeast. We still didn't know what we were up for. We thundered up through some cloud spots in tight formation.

At around 12,000 feet I turned on oxygen. Above

[233]

the immediate cloud level the weather got cold and I glanced over the instrument panel, making sure everything was shipshape. Aside from the temperature, everything was O.K. I was glad I had worn a fur-lined Irving suit and hoped we collected no ice coating on the wings.

For perhaps fifteen minutes we cruised, and I was beginning to wonder if we were on a mere routine patrol when operations told us we were in the vicinity of enemy aircraft. We were in open formation, a loose V, so each man could observe the sweep of sky.

Suddenly Shorty waggled his wings and at the same time I heard him order us to echelon starboard, battle formation for a port attack. I slid over and behind Andy in the "rear man Charley" spot.

There was excitement in Shorty's voice as he cried over the radio, "Bandits below to port!"

Turning the firing button, to "fire," I switched on the gunsights. Shorty flicked his wings and peeled off in a dive. Andy followed. Taking a quick glance around and not spotting any Jerry fighters, I followed Andy.

Below Shorty and Andy were six big gray Junkers 88's, streaking through cloud wisps in two V's. Shorty headed smack for the front bomber. Andy pulled out of line, going after the leader of the rear

V. I picked the one next to Shorty's target. Shorty shouted into my earphones, "Tallyho!" Into that battle cry he put his whole soul.

Our planes screamed down with wide open throttles. My thumb was tensed against the firing button. I saw Shorty open fire as he roared into the flame-spouting guns in the Junkers' blister.

My target banked under me, just a little, to throw my aim off. I shoved the stick forward, streaking down at him in an almost vertical power dive. His nose was just behind the sights. I pressed the button and felt the jar as bullets at the rate of 160 a second poured from the eight Brownings. Tracers showed the shots passing just in front of the Junkers' nose. I edged the stick to port to bring the death stream closer. Now the bullets poured into the pyrex snout. There was a flash of light, a roar and heavy jar. A cannon shell must have hit me somewhere. The flash blinded me for a moment. I knew I was catapulting right for the bomber. I gave the button one tight squeeze and pulled the Hurricane hard over to prevent a collision. The plane's scream became a groan for an instant under the strain. A black curtain dropped over my eyes.

Instinctively I straightened her out into a dive and the curtain lifted as a cloud came up and smacked me in the face. You don't realize how fast you are rocketing until you hit a cloud.

Wham, I was through it. There, like a motion picture suddenly flashed on a screen were great factories on the edge of a city. A dark cloud loomed up and I swerved to miss it. As I caught the menacing glint of a steel cable, I realized with a shock it wasn't a cloud, but a barrage balloon.

Quickly I eased off the throttle and hauled on the stick, bringing her out of the dive slowly. There on the starboard side just in front of the windscreen was a nasty gash. That was where the cannon shell exploded. It had missed me a scant foot.

About the same level and a couple of miles to port was another aircraft. On her flank was an R.A.F. bull's-eye. Then I identified her as a Hurricane. It must be Shorty or Jim and the sight of a friendly plane was most pleasant. You don't often spot your buddies in the air after a combat and it's mighty lonely—and none too healthy—heading home by yourself. Scanning the sky for more balloons, I swerved toward the aircraft, wondering if there were any more deadly cables near by. When you are traveling fast, you often can't spot them.

Now I saw the other aircraft's single fin and rudder, or rather where they had been. They were

[236]

almost completely shot away. The single fin is the upright stationary fin to which the rudder is attached. I could barely spot a head, craning over the cowling. It must be Shorty. As I approached, the pilot saw me. He threw his Hurricane up in a vertical bank to turn toward me. It was the only way he could turn without his rudder.

When he was 400 yards away I lifted the starboard wing to give him a view of the R.A.F. insignia. Then I turned to come in beside him. A hand waved at me. It was Shorty. I gave him a thumbs up, flipped the radio key to send and called:

"Hello, Red One. Red Three calling. Seen anything of Shorty Keough's tail?"

Flipping the key to receive, I got the quick response, "Hello, Red Three. Red One answering. Thought you were protecting my tail. Let's go upstairs and see if we can find some more entertainment."

"Red One," I cautioned, knowing Shorty's taste for fun, "you'd better get into some clouds and head for home. You can't fight with no tail."

"Red Three, Red One answering. Only an alligator needs a tail to fight with. Formation line astern."

He gunned his Hurricane. I fell in behind him and we headed upstairs. I was itching for a chance to put some bullets where they'd do the most good. I knew Shorty was sore at the Jerry who shot him up. He had been mad at the Germans since he visited his girl at Blackpool. While he was there the Jerries dumped a lot of bombs around where his girl was staying. Under his orders she spent four nights in an air-raid shelter. He sat in a deserted taproom, even after the windows were blasted in, swearing the Jerries had tracked him down just to spoil his leave.

Above the first cumulus bank I caught a glimpse of a Messerschmitt 109 in a long, slanting dive, smoke pouring from the hatch. Shorty waved at it with clenched fist and his thumb up. Good. Apparently there was action somewhere around. If only there weren't so many damned clouds.

Atop one cloud mountain I spotted three Messerschmitt 110's, those twin-engined, combination bomber-fighters, chasing what appeared to be a badly shot up Spitfire. Shorty's port wing came up in a steep bank as he turned adroitly and headed for the Me.'s. Our aircraft roared up with motors opened wide.

The Spitfire was headed for the safety of a cloud. Shorty and I cut right across the path of the chase, both of us aiming to come into the starboard side of the closest Jerry. Keeping an eye on the aircraft, I quickly set my sights for an Me. 110.

[238]

The Spitfire pilot must have seen us for his aircraft veered toward us. Shorty's wings waggled as he tried to steer for the Jerry. He was doing a remarkable job of steering with his ailerons. We were making better than 300 miles an hour and at this speed the little guy had to throw his wings away up to make his plane change course.

I pulled up and over what was left of his tail and both of us opened fire at about the same time. The Jerry didn't like facing sixteen blazing machine guns and banked steeply to starboard. I followed him, but Shorty couldn't turn quickly enough. A last glimpse showed his starboard wing rising. He was going after the second Jerry.

I rolled over and gave the first one a quick burst before he dove away and disappeared in a cloud. Pulling the Hurricane around in a tight, fast turn, I headed for where I had last seen Shorty. The turn was just short of a blackout arc. I eased off on the stick as I felt the blood draining from my head.

There was Shorty's Hurricane in the thick of the fight, being aided by the disabled Spitfire. Two Me. 110's, despite the fact they were slower and less maneuverable than Spitfires or Hurricanes, were getting the better of it against the disabled British planes. Besides, the Me.'s carried three men and were heavily armed with cannon as well as machine guns.

Shorty was throwing his Hurricane around in a desperate effort to get one of the Me. 110's in his sights. As I pulled the teat, the auxiliary throttle, and felt the fresh surge of power, Shorty pulled over into a loop, coming down almost on the tail of one Me. Now he was chasing one and the second one was chasing him. The Spitfire tried to follow the three of them but lost ground. Suddenly one of its wings dropped off and spun away. I saw the pilot slide the hatch, stand up and get jerked out of his ship by the air blast, even before his parachute opened.

The rear Me. was giving Shorty some awful punishment. I knew he was oblivious of the rear attack and wouldn't get out of the way as long as he had the front Jerry in his sights.

The three were slanting away from me and down and I roared after them. Suddenly a black smoke trail streaked from the front Messerschmitt. It rolled over and down steeply, Shorty nearly putting his ship into a spin to follow it. He may have bagged him, or the Jerry may have been trying the old trick that was pulled on me.

Shorty's aircraft disappeared in the smoke for an instant. There he was again, still hanging on. He was

[240]

not taking chances on it being a trick. The front German plunged into a cloud and Shorty pulled up and did another quick loop, a maneuver that would black out the normal pilot. Because he was so short-coupled, he could stand it. The other Jerry kept right on diving and plunged into the cloud. Shorty followed him.

Down I went into the murk and through it. Below was water. During the dogfight we evidently had drifted over the North Sea or the English Channel. There were no aircraft visible. I glanced at my petrol gauge. It showed a mere seven gallons! Time to head for home quickly. Shorty must be almost out of petrol since he had done much more maneuvering than I.

I pulled up through the cloud again, coming into a burst of sunlight that was blinding. There, several miles to the east and some 3,000 feet above, was a twin-motored plane. Hot after it was a rudderless Hurricane. Both were streaking toward the Dutch coast. That crazy Shorty! He was too busy keeping his eyes on his gunsights to look at his petrol gauge. I never could catch them and it would be suicide to stay over the sea any longer.

Quickly I snapped the radio to send and called, omitting the formal R.T. procedure:

"Shorty, you're out of petrol! Come back!"

I flipped the key to receive. There was only silence. Desperately I called operations by its code name of the day, "Hello, Thunder. Hello, Thunder. Red Three calling. Please order Red One to corner. He's nearly out of petrol and heading east over water."

Shorty must obey if he were ordered back, for the operator was a squadron leader. I heard operations order him to "corner," code for the home airdrome. There was no response. Perhaps he already had hit the deck!

I had never felt so futile before, knowing I couldn't help him. I called operations for a vector home. Coming into the home base, I landed and taxied to the dispersal bay, and saw Andy running toward me. I was glad he had got back safely. As I slid back the hatch and climbed heavily from the office he yelled out, "Where's Shorty?"

"Flying wide open east over the North Sea with empty petrol tanks, the last I saw of him," I answered hopelessly.

After inspecting the damage to my aircraft and being assigned a new one, I entered the dispersal hut to greet a sad gang of flyers. Two hours later we received a report that Section Leader Vernon Keough was missing.

When we were relieved from duty at 8 P.M. there

was no further word. We instructed our batmen to stay by the operations room and inform us if any scrap of news came through. Knowing we had to fly tomorrow, we played ping-pong, trying to make ourselves forget. For six weeks Shorty had trained me secretly to play this game so I could beat Luke, who claimed he was pretty good. Shorty was the best player at the post, being built so close to the ground he could pick the celluloid balls off the floor. The usual joviality in the mess was missing.

Then a batman came running in.

"Gentlemen, Section Leader Keough is safe! He's on his way here."

"Where did he land?" I asked, hardly believing him.

"He lost the Nazi he was chasing in a cloud," the batman beamed.

"That's what saved him. Otherwise he'd have followed that Jerry clear to Germany," Andy thundered.

"He turned back," the batman continued, "and was forced to land on one of the airdromes near the east coast."

At 10 P.M. in walked Shorty, as dapper and cocky as ever.

"I'd have brought that Jerry down," he apologized the first thing, "if he hadn't found a cloud."

[243]

After he learned how worried we had been, he assured us, "But you knew I'd be back. I'll always come back."

We had a few days of inactivity and Shorty was beginning to bemoan the fact he hadn't been trained exclusively for night fighting. The Defiant boys still were active.

Just about the time he sold himself on applying for a night-fighter's post, we got a call for a patrol. Shorty beat Nat Maranz and me out the door. We took off into a cloudless sky and zoomed up quickly. Section Leader Keough got the vector and led us in search formation toward the North Sea. It was a perfect flying day. Level sweeps of low fog crept over northeast England far below us. It was exhilarating just to be up.

To my right I saw Nat looking over the countryside. He must be enjoying it as much as I. In front of us, his aircraft heaving and bobbing gently in the crisp air, was Shorty. I could barely see his head above the fuselage rim. His head was turning, first one way then the other. I knew he was not looking for beauty, but for trouble.

He banked to starboard and we followed in loose formation. Far below was a V of three planes, flying northwest. They were Blenheims, no doubt return-

[244]

ing from a bombing raid on France or the Low Countries.

Shorty turned again and resumed his normal course. We cruised over the North Sea. Mountains of mist, which soon would be dispelled by the morning sun, rose from it.

"Red Two and Three, Red One calling." It was Shorty's voice in the headphones. "Unidentified aircraft ahead at angels one five."

Shorty's aircraft pulled ahead and we followed closely. I scanned the sky but saw nothing as I turned the firing button and switched on the gunsights. How a fellow who had to crane his neck to see out of his plane could so readily spot airplanes was beyond me.

"It's a Dornier!" Shorty shouted in the earphones.

No time to look for the enemy now. I glanced up and through the rear mirror. It was my job to protect the formation's tail.

Shorty, with a "Tallyho!" peeled off in a steep zoom. Nat followed. Now I could see the big German bomber. It was painted gray-white on top, mist color, and was headed almost due north. Down I went after Nat in a seventy-degree screaming dive. The Dornier was spouting bullets and cannon shells up at Shorty as he streaked right into the guns. It looked as if he were going to crash into the bomber.

But he didn't change his course. The German had no time to duck for the sea. As Shorty's Hurricane came to within forty yards of it, the bomber pulled up his starboard wing, banked steeply to avoid a crash. Shorty shot by, missing the Jerry by inches.

Now Nat got in his burst. I came rocketing down for the third burst. Tracers showed bullets pouring into the metal fuselage. Then I was past the German without getting hit once.

A thousand feet below was Shorty's plane, Nat close behind. Both still were diving. Wondering why they didn't pull out, I followed them down through a thin mist cloud, with the sea plainly visible below.

In a vertical dive at 500 miles an hour Shorty's Hurricane drove for the dull green waters of the North Sea. He had better pull out in a hurry. Nat started to come out of his dive.

Then I heard a voice over the earphones. I hardly recognized it as Shorty's as chokingly he almost whispered, "Red One won't—be—back—Tallyho—boys."

In a horrifying instant I saw Shorty's plane smack the water. At the same instant over the R.T. came an explosive sound, then silence. As soon as the Hurricane hit the water it disappeared beneath a burst of foam. Maranz spiraled over the spot, marked by a widening circle of waves. Shorty must have been hit by a bullet or cannon shell.

I pulled out of my dive and circled the spot with Nat, cutting in and flying beside him. He looked over with a white face and shook his head, pointing below with his mittened hand.

It was a misty, foggy afternoon when three Hurricanes took off from our airdrome. Each aircraft carried a wreath. They flew in a V over a certain spot on the North Sea. One after another they dove, dropping the wreaths. The aircraft pulled up steeply and did a roll in final tribute to a gallant little officer. Then shroudlike mist closed in over the sea.

Chapter XV

WHAT I DID KNOW

ONE brilliantly crisp March afternoon three of us were on a patrol sweep south over the North Sea to the English Channel when we spotted, far above us and to the east, six white lines in the sky. They looked like sky-writing except that they were straight and lengthening to the west.

They were "vapor trails" made by aircraft flying in high altitudes. Friction from the fast-moving planes condensed the moisture around them, forming a thin, tubular cloud in their wake. The moisture froze before it could evaporate. The cloud stayed fixed in the atmosphere sometimes as long as an hour. Often in high-altitude combat, when aircraft are too far up to be seen from the ground, you can follow their maneuvers by the vapor trails.

Although a beautiful sight, in this instance the trails might mean enemy aircraft. We vaulted upstairs to have a look. The planes still were several miles east of us when we climbed to 26,000 feet and began making our own vapor trails. They were little ones and didn't last long. We weren't up high enough yet. The higher we went, the bigger the white clouds that seemed to pour away from our tails.

At 29,000 feet we were leaving heavy trails behind us. Now we were at the same level as the approaching aircraft. Although they were headed directly toward us and we couldn't see wing or fuselage markings, we identified them as Me. 109's from the full wing dihedral and braced tailplanes. Under two of them I could see something suspended. They must be small bombs.

As we headed toward them they circled right around and headed back the way they had come, trying to hide in their own vapor trails. With full throttle, we charged after them. It wasn't difficult to follow them as they plowed through their own vapor, spreading it out each side as a speedboat does water, and creating more vapor in their wakes.

We were gaining a bit. I saw three bombs jettisoned so that the Me.'s could pick up speed. They were still about a mile and a half away as we streaked over the French Coast. Figuring we had chased them far enough, we dropped down to have a look at an enormous quantity of what appeared to be boats lined along the coast below.

I was "rear man Charley" so I kept an eye on the Me.'s to see that they didn't try to sneak back on our tails. They apparently had made up their minds to go straight home for the vapor trails kept right on heading east.

As we leveled off at about 12,000 feet I saw literally hundreds of barges hugging piers and beaches. They were so close together you probably could have walked across them. Not far inland three long trains were moving toward the coast. We skimmed past one spot that had felt the heavy hand of British bombers. The otherwise neat scallops of barges were broken by piles of wreckage where explosives had splintered more than a score of them, tossing them on top of one another and heaving several pieces of them onto some small docks.

I saw jets of smoke below. Evidently the flak gunners were trying to bring us down. As there were no black puffs of exploding shells anywhere near by, I thought the gunners must be far off their beam.

Then I spotted a big formation of Blenheim bombers, escorted by fleets of Spitfires flying in a protective cone over them. They were the antiaircraft target. But the formation was too high for accurate aiming. It was a grand sight to see your own bombers coming over to give the Nazis a little of their own medicine.

Shortly Nazi interceptors would go up and attempt an attack on the bombers. I pitied any of them that tried to dive through that cone of sleek Spitfires. The usual tactics of the Me. 109's and Heinkel 113's were to try and coax a section or two of Spitfires into combat, thus leaving an opening for other Jerry fighters to get at the bombers. But the Spitfire pilots didn't attack unless they or the bombers were attacked directly. Their job wasn't to bring down enemy fighters, but to see that the bombers got to their objective and safely home. Later the Eagle Squadron was assigned to convoy bombers during these daylight sweeps.

We got back to the station to learn that Jim McGinnis had just been killed. He had just taken off with two new members of the squadron and when his aircraft was only 350 feet off the ground it had rolled over, belly up, and hurtled into some trees. The aircraft caught fire and all 9,600 rounds of ammunition had gone off. What had caused the plane to invert I don't believe ever was learned.

March, as February had been, was a tough month for the Eagle Squadron. Paul Anderson, who had been a pal of Bud Orbison, both being from Sacramento, was killed by a bomb in London.

I felt pretty low the day I visited the Eagle Squadron cemetery for Jim's funeral and saw the growing number of graves. For a moment I wondered what was happening to the old squadron. Then I realized that instead of dying, it actually was growing stronger. It had built up to thirty-two men. More fellows were coming over from the United States and there was talk about organizing a second all-American Eagle Squadron.

And the squadron was doing things. Gus Daymond already had brought down German planes. Pete Peterson was showing the leadership and flying skill that marked him as a coming ace.

I didn't know then, of course, that after the squadron had been operational for a year Gus and Pete would be the only two members of the original Eagle Squadron still in action. I didn't know, either, that both of them would be "aces," a term used for a combat flyer who has brought down five enemy planes, that both would have been decorated with the Distinguished Flying Cross, that Gus would be a flight lieutenant and Pete the squadron leader of the Eagles. Also, I did not know that there would be a third Eagle Squadron as well as a second and that some 150 Americans would be in these squadrons to carry on gloriously the traditions of the Lafayette Escadrille.

But what I did know as I stood in the cemetery was that an immortal message delivered by an American President long ago at another war cemetery applied to this hallowed ground. I didn't recall the exact words, but later I looked them up. They ran:

"It is for us the living, rather, to be dedicated here to the unfinished work which they who fought here have thus far so nobly advanced. It is rather for us to be here dedicated to the great task remaining before us—that from these honored dead we take increased devotion to that cause for which they gave their last full measure of devotion."

Chapter XVI

BIG FLAP

ONE afternoon as the gray light over the airdrome was thickening into dusk, Luke and I had just settled down to a typical friendly argument with a British pilot over the merits of various fighter planes when our talk was cut short by the loud speaker:

"Squadron ——, Red and Blue sections. Squadron ——, Green and White sections. Scramble!"

The Britisher smiled hopefully as he jumped up with, "Twelve of us going up. It's a big flap this time!" It had to be or they wouldn't risk sending us aloft so late in the day.

A dozen of us, six Americans and six Britishers, ran out to our aircraft. The Britishers were the Spitfire boys. I climbed into a new Hurricane. The motor on mine was being overhauled. I was a little dubious about the new plane, not knowing its little habits. Each aircraft has its own.

Both sections of the Spitfire squadron roared down the runway and the six planes took off as one. Those boys were beautiful formation flyers.

M., the leader of our flight, taxied out, the two aircraft in his section coming into a vic behind him. They took off and we followed immediately. In two tight vics, one right behind the other, we thundered upward into a cloud canopy which was made almost as black as night by coal smoke from factories. M.'s tail was directly under my propeller. It was so dark I couldn't see his wings.

On the radio I heard him get vectored to 270, operations adding, "Buster!" This meant step on it. M.'s tail drew away. I pulled the teat a little and came up close. Our planes were just inches apart. I felt a vibration. Must be Luke's wing tip against mine. Visibility was too poor now for him to see me motion him back. A quick glance showed Luke's wing edging back a little. He had felt the impact too.

Operations called again, reporting, "Angels two five. Many, many bandits!"

Many enemy aircraft at 25,000 feet! The altimeter read 12,000 feet. I turned on the oxygen, spinning the dial to 17,000 feet.

I fervently hoped operations was vectoring us right. There were two balloon barrages in this vi-

[255]

cinity and it would be just too bad if we got snagged in one. I wondered if my guns were hot enough to fire, if the rest of the boys in the formation were getting the right information, and understood it, and if the motor, this new motor I'd never tried out before, would respond to the big job required of it in combat. You don't actually worry about these things, but you can't help their flashing through your mind.

Suddenly we burst through the black cloud bank into the brilliance of the evening sky. The sun was almost resting on a crimson mattress. Admiration of the beauty about us was cut off by operations:

"Hello, Red Leader. Locust Control calling. Are you receiving me?"

"Hello, Locust Control. Red Leader answering. Receiving you loud and clear. Over," M. answered.

"Hello, Red Leader. Locust Control calling. Bandits five miles to port at angels two zero. Buster!"

We were flying at 22,000 feet. We didn't see them. They must be under that big ragged hole in the clouds. M. called for echelon starboard. Our Hurricanes moved into single file, each plane to the right of the plane in front. M. banked to the left and one after the other we followed.

There were the Jerries! Three swarms of black specks several thousand feet above. They were the

[256]

Messerschmitt fighter convoys. They were always above us. I could just make them out. There must be fifty of them. But we were not looking for them. I glanced below as we roared over the big cloud rift. There was our quarry. Fifteen big murky green bombers. Junker 88's, flying in three stepped-up, line-astern formations. It was the toughest formation to attack because the bombers were flying in three groups, one above the other. In our dive we had to run the gantlet of cannon and machine-gun blasts from each level.

Far off in the golden mist I saw other clusters of planes. They must be over the English Channel. I couldn't tell whether they were German or British. Behind us were more planes. They were closer and camouflaged green and tan. They were Spitfires from some other airdrome, a welcome addition to the sky picture!

M. was angling for a beam attack. I set and turned on the gunsight, caught a glimpse of the reassuring glow and set the button in firing position. Striking down at the side of the bombers would give us the biggest target. Besides, the Ju.88's weren't armored there. There was a cool feeling in my stomach and my mouth got very dry. The dryness may have been caused by the oxygen. I was taking in deep breaths of

[257]

it. There was a swarm of Messerschmitt 109's directly overhead, and following us like hawks stalking their prey. They wouldn't dive until we did. Then they would be on our tail in a flash. I could see in the gathering dusk the black crosses on the underside of their square-cut wings.

Suddenly M. waggled his wings and peeled off, zooming down in a sixty-degree power dive with a "Tallyho!" Number two and number three followed screaming after him. I pulled the teat wide open and shoved the stick from me. The Hurricane jumped ahead and shrieked downstairs. The three Hurricanes in front broke formation and leveled off, each picking a separate target. I came out of my dive and got a bomber in the sights, the front Jerry in the middle formation. We must pick off the front bombers, for in one of them was the flight leader. If we got him, the rest of the formation would turn for home. But so long as he was still in action, they would keep right on to their objective.

Over the whining crescendo of airplane motors I heard in the earphones a "Yipee! Hi—Yoooo-oo!" It was one of our boys giving his cowboy battle yell. He had forgotten and left his radio on send, so we heard him.

As we roared in on them, the bombers didn't try

[258]

to get out of the way. I was watching for some evasive action to throw our aim off. My target loomed larger and larger in the sights as I started rolling over. His murky camouflaging almost blended with the darkness. My thumb was itching to press the firing button. But he was still too far away. Smoke trails poured from the bomber as the gunner opened fire at me.

The stick vibrated in my hand. Bullets from somewhere were cutting into an aileron. I could tell this because the vibration was a sideways motion. It couldn't be from a bomber below. I wasn't in range yet. The rear-view mirror showed a Messerschmitt fighter on my tail. But he was too far off to hit me. The jerking stopped. The bullets must have come from the top formation of bombers. They were almost overhead.

No time to investigate. My target was only 350 yards away. My thumb squeezed down on the firing button. Tracer smoke showed the bullets falling short and too far ahead of the pilot's cabin. I tried to pull her nose in on the target. The Hurricane responded sluggishly. From the way her starboard wing dragged I knew it was the aileron on that wing that was damaged. Probably the fabric had been shot off. I tried to keep the gunsight just ahead of his nose so the pilot would run into the hail of death. I gave him another burst. There! The tracer smoke poured into the pilot's plastic cabin. I bore down on the trigger as if trying to force more bullets into him. As I pulled down and rocketed upside down across the bomber's belly, it started to roll over. That meant I had probably got him!

As the Hurricane started into the break-away, I caught sight of two Messerschmitts on my tail. I gazed a split second too long into the rear-vision mirror. The Hurricane was roaring directly at another bomber. I hadn't spotted it in the gloom. I gave it one quick, wicked burst at almost point-blank range as the Hurricane dropped away in a sickening dive.

Just as I felt the blood draining from my head I heard a "pow"! A cannon shell from the bomber ripped through the hatch just above my head, showering the cockpit with glass and miniature shrapnel fragments. Wind whistled in the cockpit and I had to drop my head far forward so that my helmet wouldn't get ripped off by the blast.

My head and shoulders were getting unbearably heavy. Centrifugal force pulled my jaw down. Even the chin strap couldn't keep it up. I groaned trying to take a deep breath. My eyelids became too heavy to keep open and consciousness faded away.

When I came to a few seconds later there were

several screaming, diving planes around. There went a Spitfire in flames. The letters on the fuselage identified it as Hank, one of the English boys at our airdrome. Poor devil! No time for mourning now, though. It may be my turn next.

As I pulled gradually out of the dive, two streamers of fire whipped past the starboard wing. Tracers from a Messerschmitt! I had almost forgotten them. In fact, I thought my 7,000-foot dive would have carried me far away from their guns. Yes, one of them was right behind, his guns blinking like lights. There was just enough daylight left for him to see me if he was close. And he was much too close. I banked over in a tight turn. He was right after me. I twisted and writhed, but Jerry wouldn't shake loose. His bullets thrummed a tattoo somewhere on the fuselage. If an incendiary bullet started to work, it was all over. The Hurricane responded to the controls slowly because of the ruined aileron. That was why Jerry could follow me.

Only one thing was left to do—go into a spin. With the aileron damaged, the Hurricane might not come out of it, but it would be a lot better to take that chance than to sit still and get shot in the back. I gunned the throttle and jerked the stick toward me. Instantly the lift on the wings was gone. The Hurricane stalled at nearly 300 miles an hour and whipped over and down in a shrieking spin. Consciousness again left me, but I knew Jerry had zoomed past overhead.

As I began to come to it seemed as if a dozen huge propellers were spinning in my head. I shook my head to throw off the nauseating sensation and took a deep breath of oxygen. As my vision cleared, I realized that the ship was still spinning. The altimeter read 3,000 feet. I'd have to bring her out of it fast. Wondering if the bad aileron would let her come out, I shoved the stick forward and reversed the controls. Nothing happened. The altimeter showed 2,500 feet. The Hurricane was dropping at a little more than 200 miles an hour, the speedometer indicated, the spin having slowed her down.

Still holding the stick over, I grabbed for the hatch with my left hand and tried to jerk it back. It was time to jump. In an awful instant, I realized the cannon shell had jammed the hatch. Clenching my teeth and trying to swallow a panicky emotion that kept welling up in my throat, I shoved the throttle, opening it wide, and pulled the teat. It was kill or cure this time. The plane gathered speed.

Slowly—and I could hardly believe it—the controls grew firm and the spin slowed. Then it stopped as the speedometer needle climbed to 250 M.P.H.,—275—300. Quickly I eased the throttle and brought the stick back slowly on the left side. I must keep the starboard wing up. If she dove again it would be my last ride. I didn't even know if I were coming out of this dive before ramming into the ground.

The altimeter read a scant 800 feet. I was flying entirely by instruments now as it was dark everywhere except for the glowing instrument panel.

At 300 feet the Hurricane leveled off and I gasped a deep breath, lifting my head a little to let the air blast cool it. Snapping the radio switch to send, I called operations, asking for an emergency homing. I flipped the key to receive and listened, wondering whether the radio still worked. It did! The steady, unruffled voice of operations ordered:

"Talk for ten seconds."

This was to enable operations to get a bearing on me. I mumbled something into the mike, hardly aware of what it was. Then there was silence except for the roar of the motor and the wind screaming through the hatch and gun mouths.

It seemed hours, but in reality it was about fifty seconds when operations notified that I was over an airdrome. There was nothing but blackness below as I banked the Hurricane carefully in a descending turn. As the altimeter dropped below the 1,500-foot mark, a red-and-white Very rocket shot up from somewhere beneath. A welcome sight, these colors of the day! On a telegraph key I tapped out in Morse code "A" and "T," the letters of the day. The dots and dashes blinked from the amber light under my plane—that is, if they hadn't been shot off.

Apparently they hadn't for almost immediately a row of dim lights flashed on, marking the runway of the airdrome. By their yellow color I knew the lights were oil pots. This meant there was a ground haze, oil lights penetrating it better than electric lamps. Inexperienced pilots sometimes try to land on this haze—which hugs the ground to a depth of about four feet—because the top of it looks like the ground surface.

I lowered the landing wheels and flaps and nosed the Hurricane down, keeping the starboard wing up slightly. The plane slanted to the border of the runway and I edged her through the thick haze at 100 miles an hour. She hit the ground with the port wheel, bounced up, slid through the air a moment, then settled down on the runway. I shoved gently on the brakes and she eased to a stop. Suddenly I felt very much all in.

The duty pilot and a crew of mechanics and

armorers raced up to take the ship over. They pried open the badly damaged hatch and informed me that I was fifteen miles from the home airdrome. Her starboard aileron was more than half gone, part of the rudder had been shot away, three control wires were badly frayed, the cowling was smashed in near the hatch, and there were innumerable bullet holes through the fuselage and wings. Still she brought me in safely. That's a Hurricane for you!

After telephoning home, I climbed into a truck and spent a bumpy half-hour before reaching our officers' lounge. I arrived in time for a victory celebration. Pilots from our airdrome had brought down two bombers sure and one probable, as well as two fighters. The only one not there to help with the festivities was Hank. We drank a toast to his memory.

Later that night in our room Luke took Hank's photograph off the wall.

"Guess we'd better put him away until after the war," Luke said, placing the picture in his suitcase. Then he added, "This is one more casualty that is going to cost Jerry plenty!"

We solemnly shook hands on it.

Chapter XVII

AMERICA SETS HER SIGHTS

THIS chapter might be called an anticlimax for, just as I was beginning to see some of the action that I had spent six and a half months preparing for, I was ordered off flight duty. My eardrums had been damaged by too sudden a change in atmospheric pressure in a power dive.

The Air Ministry offered me a first class ticket to America for a visit and to recuperate. It would be good to see home again, but it was tough to leave England just when I had received enough flying experience to be of some service.

My passage was arranged on a fast liner. Early one morning in March, I climbed aboard her and became one of 132 passengers bound for the United States and Canada. We hadn't been at sea long before we joined a large convoy. While our vessel was faster than most of those in the convoy, we had to travel along at the speed of the slowest freighter in the cavalcade.

We were handed leaflets entitled "Procedure for Passengers and Crew in Emergency," which gave the number of whistle blasts and klaxon toots for "emergency practice," as well as the signals for going to action stations and for abandoning ship. The vessel was well armed with antiaircraft, submarine, and machine-guns. Because of my familiarity with rapid-fire guns and German aircraft, I was asked if I would like to man a machine-gun on the bridge during emergencies. Naturally, I was glad to accept. Quite a contrast, I felt, to being a pilot in a fast Hurricane.

I got acquainted with a pilot in the Ferry Command, a fine fellow who was flying bombers over from Canada to Britain. While he thought nothing of taking a Lockheed-Hudson through nine hours of sleet and storm across the North Atlantic, to say nothing of the chance of meeting enemy aircraft, he considered traveling by ship a "risky business in war-time."

Speaking of risks, he and I got a kick out of his cabin mate, a bulky little man who tried to wear his life belt to bed with him. Unable to do this and get any sleep, the fellow folded the preserver and placed it on the bed beside him.

The fourth night out while a group of us were talking in the lounge, two long blasts came from the ship's whistle, followed by the tooting of klaxons. It was the call to action stations.

Running up to the bridge, I saw star shells bursting into the black night, fired by our naval escorts to help them sight the enemy. I presumed we were being attacked by submarines, since we must be too far out for bombers. Just after I reached the machine-gun on the bridge, I spotted a white streak in the water as it crossed our path, not 200 feet in front of the bow. It was a torpedo's wake and elongating very fast.

In a few seconds our boat shuddered from a dull explosion that lighted up the sky. About 200 yards away a freighter was breaking in two. The vessel rose in the middle, split apart and each half slid quickly into the sea. The rest of the convoy hurried on as it would be suicide to stop and hunt for survivors.

The vice-admiral in charge of the convoy, who was aboard our boat, said that we were being attacked by several submarines. There was no further activity in our immediate vicinity except now and then a former United States destroyer would go scurrying past in the darkness, occasionally dropping depth charges that "whoomed" somewhere below the ocean surface

[268]

and sent wide, squatty eruptions of water into the air.

The next excitement came more than a day later. At five o'clock in the morning we got the signals to go to battle stations. I jumped into my clothes, cursing the Nazis for continually disturbing us. On deck I nearly bumped into J. M. H., a tall English youth on his way to Canada to join the crew of a merchant ship.

"Rotten hour to have a boat drill, what?" he lied coolly to three women who were coming on deck behind me. Quite a contrast to my pilot friend's roommate who, I suppose, by this time was hiding in some lifeboat.

We heard three muffled explosions, either from torpedoes or the guns of destroyers. It still was too dark to see any action. Believing a school of submarines was following us, the vice-admiral ordered the convoy to scatter, each vessel to head for Canada on its own.

Our ship put on full speed ahead. Now we were able to travel more than twice as fast as before. During the rest of the crossing we didn't see any other ships. We finally arrived at a Canadian port after having spent a total of fifteen days at sea. I read some Canadian newspaper accounts of the submarine attacks. It was reported that five boats had been sunk. The German story, also carried in the Canadian papers, claimed twenty-two boats.

I left immediately by train for California and finally reached Pasadena. My parents came down from Oregon to see me. While resting up I took the job of technical adviser for a motion picture about the R.A.F., believing it could give Americans some appreciation of what a fighter pilot's life was like.

Coming as I did from a war zone where people were alert to danger, it was disconcerting to find that most Americans with whom I came in contact were sure "it couldn't happen here." Had some of them been able to visit Europe they would have changed their minds by realizing that war can strike with 300-mile-an-hour swiftness and almost without warning.

The recuperating was beginning to grow a little irksome. I did some flying and my ears seemed all right. Then came an opportunity to help America directly by teaching United States Army Air Corps cadets to fly. I was instructing at a Southern California airport when December 7 rolled around. Then I knew I belonged over here. April, 1942, I received a commission and was ordered to report for active duty with the U. S. Army Air Corps at Moffett

Field, California. Perhaps by the time this is published I'll be in combat again. I hope so.

That about winds up the story. As I said in the beginning, this hasn't been an account of brilliant combats and sparkling aerial craftsmanship. It's just the story of the most interesting months of my life. I hope a little of what the experience has meant to me has been captured in this book.

As for the boys in the Eagle Squadrons, it must be heartening for them to know that thousands and thousands of American pilots are taking off and following them into the bright blue battleground of this second World War, and that soon the roar of these thousands of American eagles will be heard around the world.